Date: 3/10/16

363.33 GUN

Guns and crime /

At Issue

| Guns and Crime

Other Books in the At Issue Series:

At Issue

| Guns and Crime

Noël Merino, Book Editor

GREENHAVEN PRESS
A part of Gale, Cengage Learning

Farmington Hills, Mich • San Francisco • New York • Waterville, Maine
Meriden, Conn • Mason, Ohio • Chicago

Elizabeth Des Chenes, *Director, Content Strategy*
Douglas Dentino, *Manager, New Product*

Articles in Greenhaven Press anthologies are often edited for length to meet page requirements. In addition, original titles of these works are changed to clearly present the main thesis and to explicitly indicate the author's opinion. Every effort is made to ensure that Greenhaven Press accurately reflects the original intent of the authors. Every effort has been made to trace the owners of copyrighted material.

Cover photograph reproduced by permission of Illustration Works.

LIBRARY OF CONGRESS CATALOGING-IN-PUBLICATION DATA

Guns and crime / Noël Merino, book editor.
    pages cm. -- (At issue)
    Includes bibliographical references and index.
    ISBN 978-0-7377-7171-8 (hardcover) -- ISBN 978-0-7377-7172-5 (pbk.)
    1. Gun control--United States. 2. Firearms and crime--United States. I. Merino,
    Noël.
    HV7436.G87739 2015
    364.2—dc23
                                                            2014027268

Printed in the United States of America
1 2 3 4 5 6 7 18 17 16 15 14

Contents

Introduction

The United States has less than 5 percent of the world's population, yet it has between a third and a half of the world's civilian-owned guns, according to the Small Arms Survey, an independent research project at the Graduate Institute of International and Development Studies in Switzerland. It has the highest gun ownership rate in the world, with approximately 270 million civilian firearms, an average of eighty-nine guns for every one hundred people. The second-highest gun ownership rate is in Yemen, with fifty-five guns for every one hundred people.

Nonetheless, the United States has nowhere near the highest rate of homicide by firearms: topping that list are Honduras, El Salvador, Jamaica, Venezuela, and Guatemala. Whereas Honduras has a gun homicide rate of sixty-eight per one hundred thousand people, the United States has a gun homicide rate of only about three per one hundred thousand people, with more than two dozen countries having a higher rate. Still, the United States is notable among other developed, wealthy countries for having such a high rate. Ireland, for instance, has a rate of approximately 0.5, Australia a rate of 0.14, and France a rate of 0.06.

According to the National Crime Victimization Survey, in 2011 in the United States, 467,321 persons were victims of a crime committed with a firearm. In that same year, data collected by the US Federal Bureau of Investigation (FBI) show that guns were used in 68 percent of murders, 41 percent of robberies, and 21 percent of aggravated assaults. The homicides in the United States committed with firearms mainly involve handguns. Gun-related homicide is most common among gangs and as part of committing another felony, such as rape, robbery, and kidnapping.

Although guns can be purchased at retail stores, pawn shops, flea markets, and gun shows, the Bureau of Justice Statistics found that among prison inmates who used, carried, or possessed a firearm when they committed their crime, only 11 percent obtained their firearm from such legal channels. Most of the inmates, 40 percent, report that they obtained the gun illegally—off the street or from a theft. Almost as many, 37 percent of the inmates, say they obtained the gun from a family member or a friend. Guns are easily available in several legal and illegal venues in the United States, with the Second Amendment protecting the right to legally own guns.

The Second Amendment was adopted in 1791 as part of the Bill of Rights of the US Constitution. It reads: "A well regulated Militia, being necessary to the security of a free State, the right of the people to keep and bear Arms, shall not be infringed." There has been much debate about the meaning of the Second Amendment; in particular, whether the right identified refers to an individual right to have arms or a collective right (of the military, for instance) to have arms. Legally, there is no debate anymore, as the US Supreme Court has been very clear in recent cases that the right identified in the Second Amendment covers an individual right to bear arms.

The landmark *District of Columbia v. Heller* case, decided in 2008, solidified this understanding of the Second Amendment. In its opinion, written by Justice Antonin Scalia, the court stated: "It was plainly the understanding in the post-Civil War Congress that the Second Amendment protected an individual right to use arms for self-defense." The Court did, however, note that there may be certain restrictions on gun ownership: "Like most rights, the right secured by the Second Amendment is not unlimited." In this particular case, the Court concluded that although "nothing in our opinion should be taken to cast doubt on longstanding prohibitions on the possession of firearms by felons and the mentally ill, or laws forbidding the carrying of firearms in sensitive places such as schools and government buildings, or laws imposing conditions and qualifications on the commercial sale of arms," a handgun ban is unconstitutional since "handguns are the most popular weapon chosen by Americans for self-defense in the home, and a complete prohibition of their use is invalid."

Although the meaning of the Second Amendment is no longer a subject of widespread debate, the extent to which gun ownership ought to be managed and restricted constitutes an ongoing controversy. The Gun Control Act of 1968 limited the legal interstate transfer of weapons and established limits on gun ownership, forbidding the sale of guns to certain criminals, unlawful drug users, the mentally "defective," and illegal immigrants, among others. The Brady Handgun Violence Prevention Act of 1993 created a national background check system to prevent firearm sales to prohibited persons.

Many of the current restrictions and proposed new restrictions—such as the proposal to require private sellers to conduct background checks on guns sold at gun shows—are opposed by gun rights activists. They claim that restrictions simply hinder law-abiding citizens and do nothing to prevent crime. The statistics cited above regarding prison inmates would seem to partially bear this out—there is no shortage of ways to acquire guns illegally, as criminals often do. Yet, proponents of more gun control argue that greater restrictions on the acquisition of firearms will keep guns out of the hands of criminals and the mentally unstable, protecting society from crime. This debate about gun control is one of many controversies explored in the viewpoints included in *At Issue: Guns and Crime*.

1

Gun Crime and Violence Have Declined in Recent Years

Michael Planty and Jennifer L. Truman

Michael Planty is chief of the Victimization Statistics Unit and Jennifer L. Truman is a statistician with the Bureau of Justice Statistics in the US Department of Justice.

In the United States, there are currently about half a million violent crimes committed with firearms each year, where homicide accounts for approximately eleven thousand of those crimes. Whereas the majority of homicides are committed with a firearm, less than 10 percent of nonfatal violence involves a gun. Sex, race, age, and geographic location all impact the likelihood of gun violence. Most offenders of nonfatal gun violence are known to the victims and many victims of nonfatal gun violence do not report the crime.

In 2011, a total of 478,400 fatal and nonfatal violent crimes were committed with a firearm. Homicides made up about 2% of all firearm-related crimes. There were 11,101 firearm homicides in 2011, down by 39% from a high of 18,253 in 1993. The majority of the decline in firearm-related homicides occurred between 1993 and 1998. Since 1999, the number of firearm homicides increased from 10,828 to 12,791 in 2006 before declining to 11,101 in 2011.

Michael Planty and Jennifer L. Truman, "Firearm Violence, 1993–2011," US Department of Justice, Office of Justice Programs, Bureau of Justice Statistics, vol. NCJ 241730, May 2013, pp. 1–10, 12, www.bjs.gov.

Statistics About Firearm Violence

Nonfatal firearm-related violent victimizations against persons age 12 or older declined 70%, from 1.5 million in 1993 to 456,500 in 2004. The number then fluctuated between about 400,000 to 600,000 through 2011. While the number of firearm crimes declined over time, the percentage of all violence that involved a firearm did not change substantively, fluctuating between 6% and 9% over the same period. In 1993, 9% of all violence was committed with a firearm, compared to 8% in 2011.

The primary source of information on firearm-related homicides was obtained from mortality data based on death certificates in the National Vital Statistics System of the National Center for Health Statistics (NCHS), Centers for Disease Control and Prevention's (CDC) Web-based Injury Statistics Query and Reporting System (WISQARS). These mortality data include causes of death reported by attending physicians, medical examiners, and coroners, and demographic information about decedents reported by funeral directors who obtain that information from family members and other informants. The NCHS collects, compiles, verifies, and prepares these data for release to the public.

Handguns accounted for the majority of both homicide and nonfatal firearm violence.

The estimates of nonfatal violent victimization are based on data from the Bureau of Justice Statistics' (BJS) National Crime Victimization Survey (NCVS), which collects information on nonfatal crimes against persons age 12 or older reported and not reported to the police from a nationally representative sample of U.S. households. Homicide rates are presented per 100,000 persons and the nonfatal victimization rates are presented per 1,000 persons age 12 or older. Additional information on firearm violence in this report comes from the School-Associated Violent Deaths Surveillance Study (SAVD), the [Federal Bureau of Investigation] FBI's Supplemental Homicide Reports (SHR), the Survey of Inmates in State Correctional Facilities (SISCF), and the Survey of Inmates in Federal Correctional Facilities (SIFCF). Each source provides different information about victims and incident characteristics. Estimates are shown for different years based on data availability and measures of reliability. . . .

From 1993 to 2011, about 60% to 70% of homicides were committed with a firearm. Over the same period, between 6% and 9% of all nonfatal violent victimizations were committed with a firearm, with about 20% to 30% of robberies and 22% to 32% of aggravated assaults involving a firearm.

Handguns accounted for the majority of both homicide and nonfatal firearm violence. A handgun was used in about 83% of all firearm homicides in 1994, compared to 73% in 2011. Other types of firearms, such as shotguns and rifles, accounted for the remainder of firearm homicides. For nonfatal firearm violence, about 9 in 10 were committed with a handgun, and this remained stable from 1994 to 2011.

The Impact of Sex, Race, and Age

In 2010, the rate of firearm homicide for males was 6.2 per 100,000, compared to 1.1 for females. Firearm homicide for males declined by 49% (from 12.0 per 100,000 males in 1993 to 6.2 in 2010), compared to a 51% decline for females (from 2.3 per 100,000 females in 1993 to 1.1 in 2010). The majority of the decline for both males and females occurred in the first part of the period (1993 to 2000). Over the more recent 10-year period from 2001 to 2010, the decline in firearm homicide for both males and females slowed, resulting in about a 10% decline each.

In 2011, the rate of nonfatal firearm violence for males (1.9 per 1,000 males) was not significantly different than the rate for females (1.6 per 1,000). From 1994 to 2011, the rate of nonfatal firearm violence for males declined 81%, from 10.1 to 1.9 per 1,000 males. During the same period, the rate of nonfatal firearm violence against females dropped 67%, from 4.7 to 1.6 per 1,000 females. As with fatal firearm violence, the majority of the decline occurred in the first part of the period. From 2002 to 2011, the rate of nonfatal firearm violence for males declined 35%, while there was no statistical change in the rate for females.

In 2010, the rate of firearm homicide for blacks was 14.6 per 100,000, compared to 1.9 for whites, 2.7 for American Indians and Alaska Natives, and 1.0 for Asians and Pacific Islanders. From 1993 to 2010, the rate of firearm homicides for blacks declined by 51%, down from 30.1 per 100,000 blacks, compared to a 48% decline for whites and a 43% decline for American Indians and Alaska Natives. Asian and Pacific Islanders declined 79% over the same period, from 4.6 to 1.0 per 100,000. Although blacks experienced a decline similar to whites and American Indians and Alaska Natives, the rate of firearm homicide for blacks was 5 to 6 times higher than every other racial group in 2010. As with other demographic groups, the majority of the decline occurred in the first part of the period and slowed from 2001 to 2010.

The rate of firearm homicide for both Hispanics and non-Hispanics was about 4 per 100,000 each in 2010. However, the Hispanic rate had a larger and more consistent decline over time. The Hispanic rate declined 54% from 1993 to 2001 and declined 34% since 2001. In comparison, the non-Hispanic rate declined more slowly, down 42% from 1993 to 2001 and down 5% since 2001.

In 2011, non-Hispanic blacks (2.8 per 1,000) and Hispanics (2.2 per 1,000) had higher rates of nonfatal firearm violence than non-Hispanic whites (1.4 per 1,000). The rate of nonfatal firearm violence for Hispanics was not statistically different from the rate for blacks. From 1994 to 2011, the rates of nonfatal firearm violence for blacks and Hispanics both declined by 83%, compared to 74% for whites.

In 2010, the rate of firearm homicide was 10.7 per 100,000 for persons ages 18 to 24, compared to 8.1 for persons ages 25 to 34 and 0.3 for persons age 11 or younger. Firearm homicide against persons ages 18 to 34 accounted for about 30% of all firearm homicides in 2010. From 1993 to 2010, the rate of homicides for persons ages 18 to 24 declined 51%, compared to a 35% decline for persons ages 25 to 34 and 50% for persons age 11 or younger.

In 2011, persons ages 18 to 24 had the highest rate of nonfatal firearm violence (5.2 per 1,000). From 1994 to 2011, the rates of nonfatal firearm violence declined for persons ages 18 to 49, with each group declining between 72% and 77%. The rate for persons ages 12 to 17 declined 88%, from 11.4 to 1.4 per 1,000.

Urban residents generally experienced the highest rate of nonfatal firearm violence.

Firearm Violence by Region

In 2010, the South had the highest rate of firearm homicides at 4.4 per 100,000 persons, compared to 3.4 in the Midwest, 3.0 in the West, and 2.8 in the Northeast.

From 1993 to 2010, the rate of firearm homicides in the South declined by 49%, compared to a 50% decline in the Northeast, a 37% decline in the Midwest, and a 59% decline in the West.

In 2011, residents in the South (1.9 per 1,000) had higher rates of nonfatal firearm violence than those in the Northeast (1.3 per 1,000). Residents in the South (1.9 per 1,000), Midwest (1.7 per 1,000), and West (1.8 per 1,000) had statistically similar rates of nonfatal firearm violence.

The publicly available National Vital Statistics System fatal data files do not contain information about the incident's urban-rural location or population size. This information is limited to nonfatal firearm victimizations. Urban residents generally experienced the highest rate of nonfatal firearm violence. In 2011, the rate of nonfatal firearm violence for residents in urban areas was 2.5 per 1,000, compared to 1.4 per 1,000 for suburban residents and 1.2 for rural residents. From 1994 to 2011, the rates of nonfatal firearm violence for all three locations declined between 76% and 78%.

In 2011, higher rates of nonfatal violence occurred in areas with a population of more than 250,000 residents than in areas with a population under 250,000. From 1997 to 2011, the rates of nonfatal firearm violence for populations between 250,000 and 499,999 and 1 million residents or more declined between 57% and 62%, compared to a 37% decline for residents living in populations between 500,000 and 999,999 residents.

The Risk of Firearm Violence

Intimate partners suffered about 4.7 million nonfatal violent victimizations in the 5-year period from 2007 through 2011, and the offender used a firearm in about 4% of these victimizations (about 195,700 incidents). Similar to intimate partner violent victimizations, offenders who were either a relative or known to the victim (e.g., a friend or acquaintance) used a firearm in about 4% to 7% of these total victimizations. In comparison, persons victimized by strangers experienced about 11 million violent victimizations, and the offender used a firearm in 11% of these victimizations.

In 2007–11, the majority of nonfatal firearm violence occurred in or around the victims home (42%) or in an open area, on the street, or while on public transportation (23%). Less than 1% of all nonfatal firearm violence occurred in schools.

The number of homicides at schools declined over time, from an average of 29 per year in the 1990s (school year 1992–93 to 1999–00) to an average of 20 per year in the 2000s (school year 2000–01 to 2009–10). Generally, homicides in schools comprised less than 2% of all homicides of youth ages 5 to 18. During the 2000s, an average of about 1,600 homicides of youth ages 5 to 18 occurred per year. The majority of homicides against youth both at school and away from school were committed with a firearm.

In 2007–11, about 23% of all nonfatal firearm victims were physically injured during the victimization. About 7% suffered serious injuries (e.g., a gunshot wound, broken bone, or internal injuries), while 16% suffered minor injuries (e.g., bruises or cuts). Of the nonfatal firearm victims who were injured, 72% received some type of care, with about 82% receiving care in a hospital or medical office.

The victim reported that the offender had fired the weapon in 7% of all nonfatal firearm victimizations. The victim suffered a gunshot wound in 28% of these victimizations.

The Victims of Firearm Violence

In 2007–11, about 61% of nonfatal firearm violence was reported to the police, compared to 46% of nonfirearm violence. Among the nonfatal firearm victimizations that went unreported in 2007–11, the most common reasons victims gave for not reporting the crime was fear of reprisal (31%) and that the police could not or would not do anything to help (27%).

In 2007–11, there were 235,700 victimizations where the victim used a firearm to threaten or attack an offender. This amounted to approximately 1% of all nonfatal violent victimizations in the 5-year period. The percentage of nonfatal violent victimizations involving firearm use in self defense remained stable at under 2% from 1993 to 2011. In 2007–11, about 44% of victims of nonfatal violent crime offered no resistance, 1% attacked or threatened the offender with another type of weapon, 22% attacked or threatened without a weapon (e.g., hit or kicked), and 26% used nonconfrontational methods (e.g., yelling, running, hiding, or arguing).

In instances where the victim was armed with a firearm, the offender was also armed with a gun in 32% of the victimizations, compared to 63% of victimizations where the offender was armed with a lesser weapon, such as a knife, or unarmed. A small number of property crime victims also used a firearm in self defense (103,000 victims or about 0.1% of all property victimizations); however, the majority of victims (86%) were not present during the incident. No information was available on the number of homicide victims that attempted to defend themselves with a firearm or by other means.

2

Many Children and Teens Are Killed or Injured by Guns Every Year

Children's Defense Fund

The Children's Defense Fund is a nonprofit child organization that advocates nationwide on behalf of children to ensure that they are always a priority.

Over two hundred children and teens die every month in the United States from guns, the majority of deaths being homicides. Black children and teens suffer a disproportionate risk of gun violence, although the majority of deaths are among white children and teens. Boys and older teenagers face the highest risk of gun violence. Guns injure over a thousand children and teens each month with the majority the result of assault, but almost one in five are accidents.

Two thousand six hundred and ninety-four children and teens died from guns in the United States in 2010.
This means:

- 1 child or teen died every 3 hours and 15 minutes.

- 7 children and teens died every day, more than 20 every three days.

- 51 children and teens died every week or five classrooms of 20 died every two weeks.

Child and Teen Gun Deaths

Even though total gun deaths dropped in 2010 for the fourth consecutive year, gun death rates remained higher than in the early 1960s.

In 2010, the rate of gun deaths in children and teens was 30 percent higher than in 1963, when data were first collected from all states.

Gun deaths in children and teens dropped 4 percent from 2009 to 2010, which meant 99 fewer children and teens were killed by guns. Both homicide and suicide gun deaths decreased in 2010: homicide deaths dropped 4 percent, from 1,855 to 1,773, and suicide deaths dropped 6 percent, from 800 to 749. In contrast accidental deaths increased 18 percent, from 114 to 134 deaths.

While gun homicide rates in children and teens have decreased in recent years, rates in 2010 remained more than three times higher than in 1963. Suicide rates in 2010 were nearly double what they had been in 1963.

Children and teen gun deaths are most likely to be homicides, in contrast to adult gun deaths which are most likely to be suicides.

Between 1963 and 2010, an estimated 166,500 children and teens died from guns.

In 2010, there were 1,773 homicide gun deaths among children and teens, 749 suicide gun deaths, 134 accidental gun deaths, and 38 deaths of undetermined intent.

Two out of three child and teen gun deaths in 2010 were homicides and a little over one out of four were suicides. In contrast, among adults two out of three deaths were suicides, and one out of three was a homicide.

Since 1963, three times more children and teens died from guns on American soil than U.S. soldiers were killed in action in wars abroad. An estimated 166,500 children and teens have died from guns since 1963.

Between 1963 and 2010, an estimated 166,500 children and teens died from guns on American soil, while 52,183 U.S. soldiers were killed in action in the Vietnam, Afghanistan, and Iraq wars combined during that same time period.

On average 3,470 children and teens every year were killed by guns during this period—the equivalent of 174 classrooms of 20 children every year.

Gun Violence and Race

Gun violence affects children of all races although Black children and teens are most at risk.

Since data collection began in 1963, Black children and teens have consistently suffered from the highest rates of gun deaths.

While Black children and teens have experienced the highest rates of gun deaths, the largest number of deaths has been among White children and teens. Out of an estimated 166,600 deaths, 53 percent were among White children and teens, and 36 percent were among Blacks the same age.

Rates of gun deaths soared in the late 1980s and early 1990s among Black children and teens, and to a lesser degree among their Asian or Pacific Islander and Hispanic counterparts.

In 2010, gun death rates among Black children and teens remained higher than in the late 1970s and early 1980s, and nearly twice as high as rates in the other race and ethnic groups. Gun death rates in 2010 were at their lowest recorded level for Asian/Pacific Islander and for Hispanic children and teens, and near the lowest recorded level for White and for American Indian/Alaska Native children and teens.

In 2010, gun deaths claimed the lives of 2,694 children and teens: 1,205 were Black, 909 White, 512 Hispanic, 41 American Indian or Alaska Native, and 27 Asian or Pacific Islander.

Black children and teens were 17 times more likely to die from a gun homicide than White children and teens.

Although Black children and teens were only 15 percent of American children and teens in 2010, they were 45 percent of child and teen gun deaths.

Black children and teens had the highest rate of gun deaths per capita, 9.4 deaths per 100,000 Black children and teens. This was 4.7 times higher than the rate for White children and teens, who had the second lowest rate of death after Asians or Pacific Islanders. American Indian or Alaska Native children and teens were also at increased risk of gun violence, with a rate of gun deaths that was 2.4 times higher than among their White peers.

Black children and teens were at increased risk of dying from a gun due to high gun homicide rates. Black children and teens were 17 times more likely to die from a gun homicide than White children and teens and 24 times more likely than their Asian or Pacific Islander peers.

American Indian or Alaska Native children and teens had the highest rate of gun suicides, 8.5 times higher than Asian or Pacific Islander children and teens and nearly twice as high as White children and teens.

Asian or Pacific Islander children and teens had the lowest rates of all types of gun deaths.

The Impact of Sex and Age

The majority of gun deaths occur in boys.

Eighty-seven percent of gun deaths occurred in boys, and 13 percent in girls in 2010.

Boys were nearly seven times more likely to be killed by gunfire than girls.

Boys had higher death rates for all types of gun deaths. They were eight times more likely than girls to die in a gun suicide, six times more likely to die in a gun homicide, and five times more likely to die a gun accident.

Older teenagers are most at risk from gun violence.

Eighty-six percent of gun deaths in 2010 occurred in 15–19 year-olds, 8 percent among 10–14 year-olds, and 3 percent each in 5–9 year-olds and children under age 5. But more children under 5 were killed by guns than law enforcement officers were killed by guns in the line of duty.

The manner of gun deaths differs according to the age of the victim. While homicides were the most common manner of gun death for all age groups, gun suicides rarely occurred in children under 10, and gun accidents were most prevalent in younger children.

Black males ages 15–19 were nearly 30 times more likely to die in a gun homicide than White males and more than three times more likely to die in a gun homicide than Hispanic males of the same age.

Child and Teen Gun Injuries

15,576 children and teens were injured by guns in 2010.

This means:

- 1 child or teen was injured every 34 minutes.

- 43 children and teens were injured every day.

- 300 children and teens were injured every week.

The estimated number of children and teens injured by guns in 2010 increased by 13 percent, with 1,785 more injuries than the year before, bringing the number of injuries up to the level last seen in 2005.

Assault and self-harm injuries increased in 2010, while accidental injuries decreased.

Seventy-eight percent of all gun injuries for children and teens in 2010 were the result of assaults (12,077 injuries), 19 percent were accidental (3,019) and three percent were self-inflicted (480).

Children of color continue to be disproportionately affected by gun violence, with Black children and teens most at risk for being injured by a gun.

In 2010, an estimated 7,232 Black, 3,571 Hispanic, and 2,839 White children and teens were injured by guns.*

Black children and teens were eight-and-a-half times more likely than their White peers and two-and-a-half times more likely than their Hispanic peers to be injured by a gun.

The rate of gun injuries increased slightly for children and teens in all race and ethnic groups between 2009 and 2010.

In 2010, 46 percent of gun injuries were among Black, 23 percent among Hispanic, and 18 percent among White children and teens.

Slightly more than half of assault gun injuries occurred in Black, and over a quarter were in Hispanic children and teens. Nearly all self-inflicted gun injuries were in White children and teens, as were over half of all accidental injuries.

Black children and teens were eight-and-a-half times more likely than their White peers and two-and-a-half times more likely than their Hispanic peers to be injured by a gun. Hispanic children and teens were over three times more likely to be injured by a gun than their White peers.

A Black was nearly 32 times more likely to be injured by a gun during an assault than a White, and two-and-a-half times more likely than a Hispanic child or teen.

---

*Another 1,584 children and teens whose race and ethnicity was "not stated" and another 349 whose race and ethnicity was categorized as "other non-Hispanic" were also estimated to be injured by guns.

Older teens are most at risk for being injured by a gun.

In 2010, the overwhelming majority of gun injuries happened to older teens, with 89 percent of gun injuries in teens ages 15–19.

Seventy percent of gun injuries were assault injuries of teens ages 15–19. Sixteen percent of gun injuries were accidental gun injuries for teens ages 15–19.

Boys are more likely to be injured by a gun.

Boys made up 88 percent of all gun injuries among ages 0–19 in 2010. They comprised 90 percent of gun assault injuries, 88 percent of accidental gun injuries and 76 percent of all self-inflicted gun injuries.

Boys were more than seven times more likely to be injured by a gun than girls.

3

Guns, Mental Illness, and Newtown

David Kopel

David Kopel is an associate policy analyst at the Cato Institute, research director at the Independence Institute, and an adjunct professor of advanced constitutional law at Denver University, Sturm College of Law.

The rate of random mass shootings in the United States has increased in recent decades, although the overall homicide rate has fallen. The increase is not due to gun-control laws, which have become stricter. Possible causes include the media coverage of mass shootings and possible copycat crimes; the deinstitutionalization of the mentally ill; and the creation of "pretend" gun-free zones, where mass shooters are assured an unarmed population without any kind of armed security.

Has the rate of random mass shootings in the United States increased? Over the past 30 years, the answer is definitely yes. It is also true that the total U.S. homicide rate has fallen by over half since 1980, and the gun homicide rate has fallen along with it. Today, Americans are safer from violent crime, including gun homicide, than they have been at any time since the mid-1960s.

Mass shootings, defined as four or more fatalities, fluctuate from year to year, but over the past 30 years there has been no long-term increase or decrease. But "random" mass shootings, such as the horrific crimes last Friday in Newtown, Conn., have increased.

Alan Lankford of the University of Alabama analyzed data from a recent New York Police Department study of "active shooters"—criminals who attempted to murder people in a confined area, where there are lots of people, and who chose at least some victims randomly. Counting only the incidents with at least two casualties, there were 179 such crimes between 1966 and 2010. In the 1980s, there were 18. In the 1990s, there were 54. In the 2000s, there were 87.

If you count only such crimes in which five or more victims were killed, there were six in the 1980s and 19 in the 2000s.

Why the increase? It cannot be because gun-control laws have become more lax. Before the 1968 Gun Control Act, there were almost no federal gun-control laws. The exception was the National Firearms Act of 1934, which set up an extremely severe registration and tax system for automatic weapons and has remained in force for 78 years.

Nor are magazines holding more than 10 rounds something new. They were invented decades ago and have long been standard for many handguns. Police officers carry them for the same reason that civilians do: Especially if a person is attacked by multiple assailants, there is no guarantee that a 10-round magazine will end the assault.

The 1980s were much worse than today in terms of overall violent crime, including gun homicide, but they were much better than today in terms of mass random shootings. The difference wasn't that the 1980s had tougher controls on so-called "assault weapons." No assault weapons law existed in the U.S. until California passed a ban in 1989.

Connecticut followed in 1993. None of the guns that the Newtown murderer used was an assault weapon under Connecticut law. This illustrates the uselessness of bans on so-called assault weapons, since those bans concentrate on guns' cosmetics, such as whether the gun has a bayonet lug, rather than their function.

Firearms are the most heavily regulated consumer product in the United States.

What some people call "assault weapons" function like every other normal firearm—they fire only one bullet each time the trigger is pressed. Unlike automatics (machine guns), they do not fire continuously as long as the trigger is held. They are "semi-automatic" because they eject the empty shell case and load the next round into the firing chamber.

Today in America, most handguns are semi-automatics, as are many long guns, including the best-selling rifle today, the AR-15, the model used in the Newtown shooting. Some of these guns look like machine guns, but they do not function like machine guns.

Back in the mid-1960s, in most states, an adult could walk into a store and buy an AR-15 rifle, no questions asked. Today, firearms are the most heavily regulated consumer product in the United States. If someone wants to purchase an AR-15 or any other firearm, the store must first get permission for the sale from the FBI or its state counterpart. Permission is denied if the buyer is in one of nine categories of "prohibited persons," including felons, domestic-violence misdemeanants, and persons who have been adjudicated mentally ill or alcoholic.

Since gun controls today are far stricter than at the time when "active shooters" were rare, what can account for the increase in these shootings? One plausible answer is the media. Cable TV in the 1990s, and the Internet today, greatly magnify the instant celebrity that a mass killer can achieve. We know that many would-be mass killers obsessively study their predecessors.

Loren Coleman's 2004 book *The Copycat Effect: How the Media and Popular Culture Trigger the Mayhem in Tomorrow's Headlines* shows that the copycat effect is as old as the media itself. Johann Wolfgang von Goethe's 1774 classic *The Sorrows of Young Werther* triggered a spate of copycat suicides all over Europe. But today the velocity and pervasiveness of the media make the problem much worse.

A second explanation is the deinstitutionalization of the violently mentally ill. A 2000 *New York Times* study of 100 rampage murderers found that 47 were mentally ill. In the *Journal of the American Academy of Psychiatry Law* (2008), Jason C. Matejkowski and his co-authors reported that 16% of state prisoners who had perpetrated murders were mentally ill.

It must be acknowledged that many of [the] attacks today unfortunately take place in pretend "gun-free zones," such as schools, movie theaters and shopping malls.

In the mid-1960s, many of the killings would have been prevented because the severely mentally ill would have been confined and cared for in a state institution. But today, while government at most every level has bloated over the past half-century, mental-health treatment has been decimated. According to a study released in July by the Treatment Advocacy Center, the number of state hospital beds in America per capita has plummeted to 1850 levels, or 14.1 beds per 100,000 people.

Moreover, a 2011 paper by Steven P. Segal at the University of California, Berkeley, "Civil Commitment Law, Mental Health Services, and U.S. Homicide Rates," found that a third of the state-to-state variation in homicide rates was attributable to the strength or weakness of involuntary civil-commitment laws.

Finally, it must be acknowledged that many of these attacks today unfortunately take place in pretend "gun-free zones," such as schools, movie theaters and shopping malls. According to Ron Borsch's study for the Force Science Research Center at Minnesota State University-Mankato, active shooters are different from the gangsters and other street toughs whom a police officer might engage in a gunfight. They are predominantly weaklings and cowards who crumble easily as soon as an armed person shows up.

The problem is that by the time the police arrive, lots of people are already dead. So when armed citizens are on the scene, many lives are saved. The media rarely mention the mass murders that were thwarted by armed citizens at the Shoney's Restaurant in Anniston, Ala. (1991), the high school in Pearl, Miss. (1997), the middle-school dance in Edinboro, Penn. (1998), and the New Life Church in Colorado Springs, Colo. (2007), among others.

At the Clackamas Mall in Oregon last week, an active shooter murdered two people and then saw that a shopper, who had a handgun carry permit, had drawn a gun and was aiming at him. The murderer's next shot was to kill himself.

Real gun-free zones are a wonderful idea, but they are only real if they are created by metal detectors backed up by armed guards. Pretend gun-free zones, where law-abiding adults (who pass a fingerprint-based background check and a safety training class) are still disarmed, are magnets for evil-doers who know they will be able to murder at will with little threat of being fired upon.

People who are serious about preventing the next Newtown should embrace much greater funding for mental health, strong laws for civil commitment of the violently mentally ill—and stop kidding themselves that pretend gun-free zones will stop killers.

4

The Solution to Gun Violence Is Clear

Fareed Zakaria

Fareed Zakaria is the host of CNN's weekly news program Fareed Zakaria GPS.

There are usually three explanations given for why the United States has such a high number of gun homicides: mental disorders, popular culture, and easy access to guns. The American rate of mental disorders and the level of violence in popular culture are not distinctly different from other rich countries. However, laws controlling gun ownership are much laxer in the United States than comparable countries, and the evidence strongly supports a connection between stronger gun control and lower homicide rates.

Announcing Wednesday [December 18, 2012] that he would send proposals on reducing gun violence in America to Congress, President [Barack] Obama mentioned a number of sensible gun-control measures. But he also paid homage to the Washington conventional wisdom about the many and varied causes of this calamity—from mental health issues to school safety. His spokesman, Jay Carney, had said earlier that this is "a complex problem that will require a complex solution." Gun control, Carney added, is far from the only answer.

In fact, the problem is not complex, and the solution is blindingly obvious.

Three Explanations of Gun Crime

People point to three sets of causes when talking about events such as the Newtown, Conn., shootings [December 14, 2012]. First, the psychology of the killer; second, the environment of violence in our popular culture; and, third, easy access to guns. Any one of these might explain a single shooting. What we should be trying to understand is not one single event but why we have so many of them. The number of deaths by firearms in the United States was 32,000 last year. Around 11,000 were gun homicides.

To understand how staggeringly high this number is, compare it to the rate in other rich countries. England and Wales have about 50 gun homicides a year—3 percent of our rate per 100,000 people. Many people believe that America is simply a more violent, individualistic society. But again, the data clarify. For most crimes—theft, burglary, robbery, assault—the United States is within the range of other advanced countries. The category in which the U.S. rate is magnitudes higher is gun homicides.

The U.S. gun homicide rate is *30 times* that of France or Australia, according to the U.N. [United Nations] Office on Drugs and Crime, and 12 times higher than the average for other developed countries.

With 5 percent of the world's population, the United States has 50 percent of the guns.

So what explains this difference? If psychology is the main cause, we should have 12 times as many psychologically disturbed people. But we don't. The United States could do better, but we take mental disorders seriously and invest more in this area than do many peer countries.

Is America's popular culture the cause? This is highly un-likely, as largely the same culture exists in other rich countries. Youth in England and Wales, for example, are exposed to vir-tually identical cultural influences as in the United States. Yet the rate of gun homicide there is a tiny fraction of ours. The Japanese are at the cutting edge of the world of video games. Yet their gun homicide rate is close to zero! Why? Britain has tough gun laws. Japan has perhaps the tightest regulation of guns in the industrialized world.

The Evidence on Gun Control

The data in social science are rarely this clear. They strongly suggest that we have so much more gun violence than other countries because we have far more permissive laws than oth-ers regarding the sale and possession of guns. With 5 percent of the world's population, the United States has 50 percent of the guns.

There is clear evidence that tightening laws—even in highly individualistic countries with long traditions of gun owner-ship—can reduce gun violence. In Australia, after a 1996 ban on all automatic and semiautomatic weapons—a real ban, not like the one we enacted in 1994 with 600-plus exceptions— gun-related homicides dropped 59 percent over the next de-cade. The rate of suicide by firearm plummeted 65 percent. (Almost 20,000 Americans die each year using guns to com-mit suicide—a method that is much more successful than other forms of suicide.)

There will always be evil or disturbed people. And they might be influenced by popular culture. But how is govern-ment going to identify the darkest thoughts in people's minds before they have taken any action? Certainly those who urge that government be modest in its reach would not want gov-ernment to monitor thoughts, curb free expression, and ban the sale of information and entertainment.

Instead, why not have government do something much simpler and that has proven successful: limit access to guns. And not another toothless ban, riddled with exceptions, which the gun lobby would use to "prove" that such bans don't reduce violence.

A few hours before the Newtown murders last week, a man entered a school in China's Henan province. Obviously mentally disturbed, he tried to kill children. But the only weapon he was able to get was a knife. Although 23 children were injured, not one child died.

The problems that produced the Newtown massacre are not complex, nor are the solutions. We do not lack for answers.

What we lack in America today is courage.

5

The Dishonest Gun-Control Debate

Kevin D. Williamson

Kevin D. Williamson is the roving correspondent for the National Review.

The United States has a high homicide rate, including homicides committed with guns, but the explanation for that high homicide rate is not about guns. The majority of gun deaths are, in fact, suicides. Around the world and across the United States, strict gun control does not correlate with lower crime, nor lax gun control with high crime. What does correlate with violent crime is liberal politics, as cities around the country with high crime rates have a history of being run by liberals.

The gun-control debate is one of the most dishonest arguments we have in American politics. It is dishonest in its particulars, of course, but it is in an important sense dishonest in general: The United States does not suffer from an inflated rate of homicides perpetrated with guns; it suffers from an inflated rate of homicides. The argument about gun control is at its root a way to put conservatives on the defensive about liberal failures, from schools that do not teach to police departments that do not police and criminal-justice systems that do not bring criminals to justice. The gun-control debate is an exercise in changing the subject.

First, the broad factual context: The United States has a homicide rate of 4.8 per 100,000, which is much higher than that of most Western European or Anglosphere countries (1.1 for France, 1.0 for Australia). Within European countries, the relationship between gun regulation and homicide is by no means straightforward: Gun-loving Switzerland has a lower rate of homicide than do more tightly regulated countries such as the United Kingdom and Sweden. Cuba, being a police state, has very strict gun laws, but it has a higher homicide rate than does the United States (5.0). Other than the truly shocking position of the United States, the list of countries ranked by homicide rates contains few if any surprises.

If a gun legally sold in Indiana ends up someday being used in a crime in Chicago, then that is counted as an incidence of gun violence in Indiana, even though it is no such thing.

We hear a lot about "gun deaths" in the United States, but we hear less often the fact that the great majority of those deaths are suicides—more than two-thirds of them. Which is to say, the great majority of our "gun death" incidents are not conventional crimes but intentionally self-inflicted wounds: private despair, not blood in the streets. Among non-fatal gunshot injuries, about one-third are accidents. We hear a great deal about the bane of "assault rifles," but *all rifles combined*—scary-looking ones and traditional-looking ones alike—account for very few homicides, only 358 in 2010. We hear a great deal about "weapons of war" turning our streets into high-firepower battle zones, but this is mostly untrue: As far as law-enforcement records document, legally owned fully automatic weapons have been used in exactly two homicides in the modern era, and one of those was a police-issue weapon used by a police officer to murder a troublesome police informant.

Robert VerBruggen has long labored over the various in-flated statistical claims about the effects of gun-control poli-cies made by both sides of the debate. You will not, in the end, find much correlation. There are some places with very strict gun laws and lots of crime, some places with very liberal gun laws and very little crime, some places with strict gun laws and little crime, and some places with liberal gun laws and lots of crime. Given the variation between countries, the variation within other countries, and the variation within the United States, the most reasonable conclusion is that the most important variable in violent crime is not the regulation of firearms. There are many reasons that Zurich does not much resemble Havana, and many reasons San Diego does not re-semble Detroit.

The Left, of course, very strongly desires not to discuss those reasons, because those reasons often point to the failure of progressive policies. For this reason, statistical and logical legerdemain is the order of the day when it comes to the gun debate.

Take this, for example, from ThinkProgress's Zack Beau-champ, with whom I had a discussion about the issue on Wednesday evening: "STUDY: States with loose gun laws have higher rates of gun violence." The claim sounds like an en-tirely straightforward one. In English, it means that there is more gun violence in states with relatively liberal gun laws. But that is of course not at all what it means. In order to reach that conclusion, the authors of the study were obliged to insert a supplementary measure of "gun violence," that be-ing the "crime-gun export rate." If a gun legally sold in Indi-ana ends up someday being used in a crime in Chicago, then that is counted as an incidence of gun violence in Indiana, even though it is no such thing. This is a fairly nakedly politi-cal attempt to manipulate statistics in such a way as to at-tribute some portion of Chicago's horrific crime epidemic to peaceable neighboring communities. And even if we took the "gun-crime export rate" to be a meaningful metric, we would need to consider the fact that it accounts only for those guns sold *legally*. Of course states that do not have many legal gun sales do not generate a lot of records for "gun-crime exports." It is probable that lots of guns sold in Illinois end up being used in crimes in Indiana; the difference is, those guns are sold on the black market, and so do not show up in the records. The choice of metrics is just another way to put a thumb on the scale.

The argument that crime would be lower in Chicago if Indiana had Illinois's laws fails to account for the fact that Muncie has a pretty low crime rate under Indiana's laws, while Gary has a high rate under the same laws. The laws are a constant; the meaningful variable is, not to put too fine a point on it, *proximity to Chicago*. Statistical game-rigging is a way to suggest that Chicago would have less crime if Indiana adopted Illinois's gun laws ... except that one is left with the many other states in which Chicago's criminals might acquire guns. The unspoken endgame is having the entire country adapt Illinois's gun laws. But it is very likely that if the country did so, Chicago would still be Chicago, with all that goes along with that. Chicago has lots of non-gun murders, too.

On the political side, perhaps you have heard that the National Rifle Association is one of the most powerful and feared lobbies on Capitol Hill. What you probably have not heard is that it is nowhere near the top of the list of Washington money-movers. In terms of campaign contributions, the NRA is not in the top five or top ten or top 100: It is No. 228. In terms of lobbying outlays, it is No. 171. Unlike the National Beer Wholesalers Association or the American Federation of Teachers, it does not appear on the list of top-20 PACs. Unlike the National Auto Dealers Association, it does not appear on the list of top-20 PACs that favor Republicans. There is a lot of loose talk about the NRA buying loyalty on Capitol Hill, but the best political-science scholarship suggests that on issues such as gun rights and abortion, the donations follow the votes, not the other way around. That is not a secret: It is just something that people like Gabby Giffords would rather not admit.

The correlation between municipal liberalism and violent crime remains stronger than that of violent crime and gun restriction.

Violent crime has been on the decline throughout these United States for decades now, give or take the occasional blip. It is down in relatively high-crime cities such as Chicago and Philadelphia, too, though not as significantly. (It still amazes me that New York, the crazy Auntie Mame of American cities, has not had a Democratic mayor since the Republican watershed year of 1993.) But if you want to find large concentrations of violent crime in the United States, what you are looking for is a liberal-dominated city: Chicago, Detroit, Philadelphia, Oakland, St. Louis, Baltimore, Cleveland, Newark—all excellent places to get robbed or killed. By way of comparison, when Republican Jerry Sanders handed the mayoralty of San Diego over to Bob Filner in December, it was pretty well down toward the bottom of the rape-and-murder charts. The same can be said of New York. I agree with every word of criticism my fellow conservatives have heaped upon nanny-in-chief Michael Bloomberg, but would add this caveat: When he gets replaced by some cookie-cutter Democratic-machine liberal, we are going to miss his ridiculous, smug face. I lived for years in what once was one of the most infamously crime-ridden parts of New York, the section of the South Bronx near where the action of *Bonfire of the Vanities* is set in motion, and the worst consequences I ever experienced from wandering its streets at night were a hangover and the after-effects of an ill-considered order of cheese fries.

By way of comparison, Chicago is populated by uncontrolled criminals, and not infrequently governed by them. The state of Illinois has long failed to put career criminals away before they commit murder, as we can see from the rap sheets of those whom the state does manage to convict for homicide. Even Rahm Emanuel can see that. But still, nothing happens. Like those in Chicago, Detroits' liberals and Philadelphia's are plum out of excuses: They've been in charge for a long, long time now, and their cities are what they have made of them.

You can chicken-and-egg this stuff all day, of course: It may be that Detroit is poor, ignorant, and backward because it is run by liberals, or it may be run by liberals because it is poor, ignorant, and backward. You can point the accusatory vector of causation whichever direction you like, but the correlation between municipal liberalism and violent crime remains stronger than that of violent crime and gun restriction. It is hardly the fault of the people of Indiana that Chicago is populated by people who cannot be trusted with the ordinary constitutional rights enjoyed by free people from sea to shining sea.

But talking about what is actually wrong with Detroit, Chicago, or Philadelphia forces liberals to think about things they'd rather not think about, for instance the abject failure of the schools they run to do much other than transfer money from homeowners to union bosses. Liberals love to talk about the "root causes" of crime and social dysfunction, except when the root cause is liberalism, in which case it's, "Oh, look! A scary-looking squirrel gun!"

But the gun-control debate proceeds as though suicide and violent crime were part of a unitary phenomenon rather than separate issues with separate causes. The entire debate serves to obfuscate what ails our country rather than to clarify it.

6

Crime Soared with Mass. Gun Law

Jeff Jacoby

Jeff Jacoby is a nationally syndicated columnist for the Boston Globe.

Massachusetts enacted strict gun-control legislation in 1998, but rather than decreasing the gun crime rate, the rate increased in the ensuing thirteen years. Although proponents of gun control blame the failure of Massachusetts' legislation on the fact that neighboring states have laxer gun laws, this does not explain the increase in Massachusetts' gun crime since adopting the legislation—an increase not seen in neighboring states.

In 1998, Massachusetts passed what was hailed as the toughest gun-control legislation in the country. Among other stringencies, it banned semiautomatic "assault" weapons, imposed strict new licensing rules, prohibited anyone convicted of a violent crime or drug trafficking from ever carrying or owning a gun, and enacted severe penalties for storing guns unlocked.

"Today, Massachusetts leads the way in cracking down on gun violence," said Republican Governor Paul Cellucci as he signed the bill into law. "It will save lives and help fight crime in our communities." Scott Harshbarger, the state's Democratic attorney general, agreed: "This vote is a victory for common sense and for the protection of our children and our neighborhoods." One of the state's leading anti-gun activists, John Rosenthal of Stop Handgun Violence, joined the applause. "The new gun law," he predicted, "will certainly prevent future gun violence and countless grief."

It didn't.

Since 1998, gun crime in Massachusetts has gotten worse, not better.

The Impact of Gun Control

The 1998 legislation did cut down, quite sharply, on the legal use of guns in Massachusetts. Within four years, the number of active gun licenses in the state had plummeted. "There were nearly 1.5 million active gun licenses in Massachusetts in 1998," the AP [Associated Press] reported. "In June [2002], that number was down to just 200,000." The author of the law, state Senator Cheryl Jacques, was pleased that the Bay State's stiff new restrictions had made it possible to "weed out the clutter."

But the law that was so tough on law-abiding gun owners had quite a different impact on criminals.

Since 1998, gun crime in Massachusetts has gotten worse, not better. In 2011, Massachusetts recorded 122 murders committed with firearms, the [Boston] Globe reported this month [February 2013]—"a striking increase from the 65 in 1998." Other crimes rose too. Between 1998 and 2011, robbery with firearms climbed 20.7 percent. Aggravated assaults jumped 26.7 percent.

Don't hold your breath waiting for gun-control activists to admit they were wrong. The treatment they prescribed may have yielded the opposite of the results they promised, but they're quite sure the prescription wasn't to blame. Crime didn't rise in Massachusetts because the state made it harder for honest citizens to lawfully carry a gun; it rose because other states didn't do the same thing.

"Massachusetts probably has the toughest laws on the books, but what happens is people go across borders and buy guns and bring them into our state," rationalizes Boston Mayor Tom Menino. "Guns have no borders."

A Climbing Crime Rate

This has become a popular argument in gun-control circles. It may even be convincing to someone emotionally committed to the belief that ever-stricter gun control is a plausible path to safety. But it doesn't hold water.

For starters, why didn't the gun-control lobby warn legislators in 1998 that adopting the toughest gun law in America would do Massachusetts no good unless every surrounding state did the same thing? Far from explaining why the new law would do nothing to curb violent crime, they were positive it would make Massachusetts even safer. It was gun-rights advocates, such as state Senator Richard Moore, who correctly predicted the future. "Much of what has been said in support of this bill will not come to pass," said Moore during the 1998 debate. "The amount of crime we have now will at least continue."

But crime in Massachusetts didn't just continue, it began climbing. As in the rest of the country, violent crime had been declining in Massachusetts since the early 1990s. Beginning in 1998, that decline reversed—unlike in the rest of the country. For example, the state's murder rate (murders per 100,000 inhabitants) bottomed out at 1.9 in 1997 and had risen to 2.8 by 2011. The national murder rate, on the other hand, kept falling; it reached a new low of 4.7 in 2011. Guns-across-borders might have explained homicide levels in Massachusetts continuing unchanged. But how can other states' policies be responsible for an increase in Massachusetts homicides?

Relative to the rest of the country, or to just the states on its borders, Massachusetts since 1998 has become a more dangerous state. Economist John Lott, using FBI crime data since 1980, shows how dramatic the contrast has been. In 1998, Massachusetts's murder rate equaled about 70 percent of the rate for Vermont, New Hampshire, Maine, Connecticut, Rhode Island, and New York. Now it equals 125 percent of that rate.

Clearly something bad happened to Massachusetts 15 years ago. Blaming the neighbors may be ideologically comforting. But those aren't the states whose crime rates are up.

7

Stricter Gun Control Would Likely Lead to More Gun Violence

Jeffrey Miron

Jeffrey Miron is the director of undergraduate studies in the economics department at Harvard University and a senior fellow at the Cato Institute.

Both mild and strict limits on gun ownership are ineffective at deterring mentally ill people who are determined to inflict harm. Mild gun-control laws are easily circumvented by those determined to obtain the firearm and ammunition they desire. Furthermore, such mild laws only affect law-abiding citizens who are inconvenienced by such ineffective laws. Strict limits on guns—approaching prohibition—deter only responsible gun ownership, resulting in a large black market in guns and armed criminals.

The atrocity committed last weekend [January 8, 2011] in Tucson, Arizona, by alleged perpetrator Jared Loughner has predictably generated calls for new gun-control laws in the U.S.

Some want bans on the extended-capacity ammunition clips that allowed Loughner to fire more than 30 shots from his Glock semi-automatic pistol without reloading. Others want improved background screening to prevent mentally unstable individuals from purchasing guns.

Would these or other laws prevent incidents like the Arizona shooting? Probably not. And such laws, along with existing gun controls, not only harm responsible gun owners but may even increase violence.

The Ineffectiveness of Gun Control

Gun-control laws fall into two main categories. Most in the U.S. are in and of themselves mild: They permit legal gun ownership for most people in most instances, while imposing modest costs on legitimate gun owners. Examples include criminal-background checks, waiting periods to purchase a gun, minimum purchase ages, and the like.

These kinds of laws, however, are unlikely to deter someone like Loughner, who appears to have contemplated and planned his attack for a long time. The reason is simple: These laws are readily circumvented.

Gun controls, even mild ones, do have adverse consequences.

Consider, for example, a ban on extended-capacity ammunition clips. If these had been unavailable, Loughner could still have carried out his attack with a 10-bullet clip, and he might have aimed more carefully knowing he had less ammunition. Loughner could have brought several guns, allowing him to continue firing without interruption. Loughner could have purchased extended-ammo clips that were sold before a ban took effect (especially since the prospect of bans stimulates sales in advance of implementation). Or he could have bought a black-market clip, perhaps just by placing a classified advertisement.

Similar difficulties confront the use of background checks designed to prevent the mentally unstable from buying guns.

The U.S. already has such a system, but it wouldn't have stopped Loughner from buying a gun because it only applies when a court has decreed a person to be mentally unfit, which hadn't occurred in Loughner's case.

Even a broader definition of mentally unfit probably wouldn't deter someone determined to commit violence. No matter how broad the definition, this approach does nothing to close the multiple avenues whereby anyone with sufficient cash can purchase a gun and ammunition.

The Consequences of Gun Control

Gun controls like those being proposed may, on occasion, prevent horrific events like the Tucson shooting or at least reduce their harm, but in all likelihood only rarely. Avoiding a few such incidents is surely better than avoiding none, so these controls would make sense if they had no negatives of their own.

But gun controls, even mild ones, do have adverse consequences.

Comparisons between states and countries . . . provide no consistent support for the claim that gun controls lower violence.

At a minimum, these laws impose costs on people who own and use guns without harming others, whether for hunting, collecting, target practice, self-defense, or just peace of mind. The inconvenience imposed by bans on extended-ammunition clips or waiting periods to buy a gun might seem trivial compared with the deaths and injuries that occur when someone like Loughner goes on a rampage. And if the only negative from these controls were such inconveniences, society might reasonably accept that cost, assuming these controls prevent some acts of violence.

But mild controls don't always stay mild; more often, they evolve into strict limits on guns, bordering on outright prohibition. And this isn't just slippery-slope speculation; a century ago most countries had few gun controls, yet today many have virtual bans on private ownership. Some of these countries (the U.K. [United Kingdom] and Japan) have low violence rates that might seem to justify strict controls, yet others experience substantial or extreme violence (Brazil and Mexico).

More broadly, comparisons between states and countries—as well as social-science research—provide no consistent support for the claim that gun controls lower violence.

The Folly of Gun Prohibition

Strict controls and prohibition, moreover, don't eliminate guns any more than drug prohibition stops drug trafficking and use. Prohibition might deter some potential gun owners, but mainly those who would own and use guns responsibly.

Thus the classic slogan—when guns are outlawed, only outlaws will have guns—isn't only a word play; it is a fundamental insight into the folly of gun prohibition. Such an approach means the bad guys are well-armed while law-abiding citizens are not.

Even if strict controls or prohibition had prevented Loughner from obtaining a gun, he might have still carried out a violent attack. Timothy McVeigh's 1995 Oklahoma City bombing, which killed 168 people, illustrates perfectly that a determined lunatic has multiple ways to inflict harm.

Beyond being ineffective, gun prohibition might even increase violence by creating a large black market in guns. So if gun laws follow the path of drug laws, we can expect more violence under gun prohibition than in a society with limited or no controls.

The sad reality is that every society has a few people whose mental instabilities cause serious harm to others. This is tragic, but it doesn't justify ineffective and possibly counter-productive attempts to prevent such harm.

8

Gun Ownership with Stricter Controls Could Reduce Gun Violence

Jeffrey Goldberg

Jeffrey Goldberg is a staff writer for The Atlantic.

Further gun-control measures in the United States will have limited effects because of the hundreds of millions of guns that already exist in private hands. The debate now is about the impact of law-abiding citizens carrying concealed weapons. Although antigun activists claim that concealed-carry laws would increase violence, there is no evidence that they do. Situations such as shootings on campus raise the question of whether properly trained students carrying firearms could actually decrease the possibility of and impact of such shootings.

According to a 2011 Gallup poll, 47 percent of American adults keep at least one gun at home or on their property, and many of these gun owners are absolutists opposed to any government regulation of firearms. According to the same poll, only 26 percent of Americans support a ban on handguns.

The Call for Gun Control

To that 26 percent, American gun culture can seem utterly inexplicable, its very existence dispiriting. Guns are responsible for roughly 30,000 deaths a year in America; more than half of those deaths are suicides. In 2010, 606 people, 62 of them children younger than 15, died in accidental shootings.

[Gun-control activist Tom] Mauser expresses disbelief that the number of gun deaths fails to shock. He blames the American attachment to guns on ignorance, and on immaturity. "We're a pretty new nation," he told me. "We're still at the stage of rebellious teenager, and we don't like it when the government tells us what to do. People don't trust government to do what's right. They are very attracted to the idea of a nation of individuals, so they don't think about what's good for the collective."

Mauser said that if the United States were as mature as the countries of Europe, where strict gun control is the norm, the federal government would have a much easier time curtailing the average citizen's access to weapons. "The people themselves would understand that having guns around puts them in more danger."

Gun-control efforts . . . would only have a modest impact on the rate of gun violence in America.

There are ways, of course, to make it at least marginally more difficult for the criminally minded, for the dangerously mentally ill, and for the suicidal to buy guns and ammunition. The gun-show loophole could be closed. Longer waiting periods might stop some suicides. Mental-health professionals could be encouraged—or mandated—to report patients they suspect shouldn't own guns to the FBI [Federal Bureau of Investigation]-supervised National Instant Criminal Background Check System, although this would generate fierce opposition from doctors and patients. Background checks, which are conducted by licensed gun shops, have stopped almost 1 million people from buying guns at these stores since 1998. (No one knows, of course, how many of these people gave up their search for a gun, and how many simply went to a gun show or found another way to acquire a weapon.)

Other measures could be taken as well. Drum-style magazines like the kind James Holmes had that night [July 20, 2012] in Aurora [Colorado], which can hold up to 100 rounds of ammunition and which make continuous firing easy, have no reasonable civilian purpose, and their sale could be restricted without violating the Second Amendment rights of individual gun owners.

The Number of Guns in America

But these gun-control efforts, while noble, would only have a modest impact on the rate of gun violence in America.

Why?

Because it's too late.

There are an estimated 280 million to 300 million guns in private hands in America—many legally owned, many not. Each year, more than 4 million new guns enter the market. This level of gun saturation has occurred not because the anti-gun lobby has been consistently outflanked by its adversaries in the National Rifle Association [NRA], though it has been. The NRA is quite obviously a powerful organization, but like many effective pressure groups, it is powerful in good part because so many Americans are predisposed to agree with its basic message.

America's level of gun ownership means that even if the Supreme Court—which ruled in 2008 that the Second Amendment gives citizens the individual right to own firearms, as gun advocates have long insisted—suddenly reversed itself and ruled that the individual ownership of handguns was illegal, there would be no practical way for a democratic country to locate and seize those guns.

The Debate About Gun Ownership

Many gun-control advocates, and particularly advocates of a total gun ban, would like to see the United States become more like Canada, where there are far fewer guns per capita and where most guns must be registered with the federal government. The Canadian approach to firearms ownership has many attractions—the country's firearm homicide rate is one-sixth that of the U.S. But barring a decision by the American people and their legislators to remove the right to bear arms from the Constitution, arguing for applying the Canadian approach in the U.S. is useless.

Even the leading advocacy group for stricter gun laws, the Brady Campaign to Prevent Gun Violence, has given up the struggle to convince the courts, and the public, that the Constitution grants only members of a militia the right to bear arms. "I'm happy to consider the debate on the Second Amendment closed," Dan Gross, the Brady Campaign's president, told me recently. "Reopening that debate is not what we should be doing. We have to respect the fact that a lot of decent, law-abiding people believe in gun ownership."

Today, the number of concealed-carry permits is the highest it's ever been, at 8 million, and the homicide rate is the lowest it's been in four decades.

Which raises a question: When even anti-gun activists believe that the debate over private gun ownership is closed; when it is too late to reduce the number of guns in private hands—and since only the naive think that legislation will prevent more than a modest number of the criminally minded, and the mentally deranged, from acquiring a gun in a country absolutely inundated with weapons—could it be that an effective way to combat guns is with more guns?

Today, more than 8 million vetted and (depending on the state) trained law-abiding citizens possess state-issued "concealed carry" handgun permits, which allow them to carry a concealed handgun or other weapon in public. Anti-gun activists believe the expansion of concealed-carry permits represents a serious threat to public order. But what if, in fact, the reverse is true? Mightn't allowing more law-abiding private citizens to carry concealed weapons—when combined with other forms of stringent gun regulation—actually reduce gun violence? . . .

The Impact of Concealed-Carry Guns

There is no proof to support the idea that concealed-carry permit holders create more violence in society than would otherwise occur; they may, in fact, reduce it. According to Adam Winkler, a law professor at UCLA [University of California, Los Angeles] and the author of *Gunfight: The Battle Over the Right to Bear Arms in America*, permit holders in the U.S. commit crimes at a rate lower than that of the general population. "We don't see much bloodshed from concealed-carry permit holders, because they are law-abiding people," Winkler said. "That's not to say that permit holders don't commit crimes, but they do so at a lower rate than the general population. People who seek to obtain permits are likely to be people who respect the law." According to John Lott, an economist and a gun-rights advocate who maintains that gun ownership by law-abiding citizens helps curtail crime, the crime rate among concealed-carry permit holders is lower than the crime rate among police officers.

Today, the number of concealed-carry permits is the highest it's ever been, at 8 million, and the homicide rate is the lowest it's been in four decades—less than half what it was 20 years ago. (The number of people allowed to carry concealed weapons is actually considerably higher than 8 million, because residents of Vermont, Wyoming, Arizona, Alaska, and parts of Montana do not need government permission to carry their personal firearms. These states have what Second Amendment absolutists refer to as "constitutional carry," meaning, in essence, that the Second Amendment is their permit.)

Many gun-rights advocates see a link between an increasingly armed public and a decreasing crime rate. "I think effective law enforcement has had the biggest impact on crime rates, but I think concealed carry has something to do with it. We've seen an explosion in the number of people licensed to carry," Lott told me. "You can deter criminality through longer sentencing, and you deter criminality by making it riskier for people to commit crimes. And one way to make it riskier is to create the impression among the criminal population that the law-abiding citizen they want to target may have a gun."

The brandishing of a gun in front of a would-be mugger or burglar is usually enough to abort a crime in progress.

Crime statistics in Britain, where guns are much scarcer, bear this out. Gary Kleck, a criminologist at Florida State University, wrote in his 1991 book, *Point Blank: Guns and Violence in America,* that only 13 percent of burglaries in America occur when the occupant is home. In Britain, so-called hot burglaries account for about 45 percent of all break-ins. Kleck and others attribute America's low rate of occupied-home burglaries to fear among criminals that homeowners might be armed. (A survey of almost 2,000 convicted U.S. felons, conducted by the criminologists Peter Rossi and James D. Wright in the late '80s, concluded that burglars are more afraid of armed homeowners than they are of arrest by the police.)

Others contend that proving causality between crime rates and the number of concealed-carry permits is impossible. "It's difficult to make the case that more concealed-carry guns have led to the drop in the national crime rate, because cities like Los Angeles, where we have very restrictive gun-control laws, have seen the same remarkable drop in crime," Winkler told me. (Many criminologists tend to attribute America's dramatic decrease in violent crime to a combination of demographic changes, longer criminal sentencing, innovative policing techniques, and the waning of the crack wars.)

But it is, in fact, possible to assess with some degree of accuracy how many crimes have been stopped because the intended victim, or a witness, was armed. In the 1990s, Gary Kleck and a fellow criminologist, Marc Gertz, began studying the issue and came to the conclusion that guns were used defensively between 830,000 and 2.45 million times each year.

In only a minority of these cases was a gun fired; the brandishing of a gun in front of a would-be mugger or burglar is usually enough to abort a crime in progress. Another study, the federal government's National Crime Victimization Survey, asked victims of crimes whether they, or someone else, had used a gun in their defense. This study came up with a more modest number than Kleck and Gertz, finding 108,000 defensive uses of firearms a year.

All of these studies, of course, have been contested by gun-control advocates. So I asked Winkler what he thought. He said that while he is skeptical of the 2.45 million figure, even the smaller number is compelling: 108,000 "would represent a significant reduction in criminal activity."

University Recommendations for Shootings

Universities, more than most other institutions, are nearly unified in their prohibition of licensed concealed-carry weapons. Some even post notices stating that their campuses are gun-free zones. At the same time, universities also acknowledge that they are unable to protect their students from lethal assault. How do they do this? By recommending measures that students and faculty members can take if confronted by an "active shooter," as in the massacre at Virginia Tech [April 16, 2007, in Blacksburg, Virginia].

These recommendations make for depressing reading, and not only because they reflect a world in which random killing in tranquil settings is a genuine, if rare, possibility. They are also depressing because they reflect a denial of reality.

Here are some of the recommendations:

- Wichita State University counsels students in the following manner: "If the person(s) is causing death or serious physical injury to others and you are unable to run or hide you may choose to be compliant, play dead, or fight for your life."

- The University of Miami guidelines suggest that when all else fails, students should act "as aggressively as possible" against a shooter. The guidelines, taken from a Department of Homeland Security directive, also recommend "throwing items and improvising weapons," as well as "yelling."

- Otterbein University, in Ohio, tells students to "breathe to manage your fear" and informs them, "You may have to take the offensive if the shooter(s) enter your area. Gather weapons (pens, pencils, books, chairs, etc.) and mentally prepare your attack."

- West Virginia University advises students that if the situation is dire, they should "act with physical aggression and throw items at the active shooter." These items could include "student desks, keys, shoes, belts, books, cell phones, iPods, book bags, laptops, pens, pencils, etc."

- The University of Colorado at Boulder's guidelines state, "You and classmates or friends may find yourselves in a situation where the shooter will accost you. If such an event occurs, quickly develop a plan to attack the shooter. . . . Consider a plan to tackle the shooter, take away his weapon, and hold him until police arrive."

It is, of course, possible to distract a heavily armed psychotic on a suicide mission by throwing an iPod at him, or a pencil. But it is more likely that the psychotic would respond by shooting the pencil thrower.

Publicly describing your property as gun-free is analogous to posting a notice on your front door saying your home has no burglar alarm.

The Dangers of Gun-Free Campuses

The existence of these policies suggests that universities know they cannot protect their students during an armed attack. (At Virginia Tech, the gunman killed 30 students and faculty members in the 10 minutes it took the police to arrive and penetrate the building he had blockaded.) And yet, these schools will not allow adults with state-issued concealed-carry permits to bring their weapons onto campus, as they would be able to almost anywhere else. "Possession or storage of a deadly weapon, destructive device, or fireworks in any form . . . is prohibited," West Virginia University's policy states.

To gun-rights advocates, these policies are absurd. "The fact that universities are providing their faculties and students with this sort of information is, of course, an admission that they can't protect them," Dave Kopel [research director of the Independence Institute] told me. "The universities are unable to protect people, but then they disable people from protecting themselves."

It is also illogical for campuses to advertise themselves as "gun-free." Someone bent on murder is not usually dissuaded by posted anti-gun regulations. Quite the opposite—publicly describing your property as gun-free is analogous to posting a notice on your front door saying your home has no burglar alarm. As it happens, the company that owns the Century 16 Cineplex in Aurora had declared the property a gun-free zone.

"As a security measure, it doesn't seem like advertising that fact is a good idea," Adam Winkler says of avowedly gun-free campuses, though he adds that "advertising a school's gun-free status does provide notice to potentially immature youth that they're not allowed to have guns."

The Concern for Campus Safety

In Colorado, the epicenter of the American gun argument, the state supreme court recently ruled that the University of Colorado must lift its ban on the carrying of concealed handguns by owners who have been licensed by local sheriffs. (The university has responded by requiring students who own guns to move to a specified housing complex.) The ruling has caused anxiety among some faculty. The chairman of the faculty assembly, a physics professor named Jerry Peterson, told the Boulder *Daily Camera*, "My own personal policy in my classes is if I am aware that there is a firearm in the class—registered or unregistered, concealed or unconcealed—the class session is immediately canceled. I want my students to feel unconstrained in their discussions."

Peterson makes two assumptions: The first is that he will know whether someone is carrying a concealed weapon in class. The second is that students will feel frightened about sharing their opinions if a gun is present. (I could find no evidence that any American educational institution has ever seen fatalities or serious gun-related injuries result from a heated classroom discussion.)

Claire Levy, a Colorado state legislator, says she intends to introduce a bill that would ban guns once again. "If discussions in class escalated," she argues, "the mere fact that someone is potentially armed could have an inhibiting effect on the classroom. This is genuinely scary to faculty members." The push to open up campuses to concealed-carry permit holders, Levy says, is motivated by ideological gun-rights advocacy, rather than an actual concern for campus safety. Guns, even those owned by licensed and trained individuals, she insists, would simply make a campus more dangerous. "American campuses are the safest places to be in the whole world," she said. "The homicide rate on campuses is a small fraction of the rate in the rest of the country. So there's no actual rational public-safety reason that anyone would need to bring a gun on campus."

However, the University of Colorado's own active-shooter recommendations state:

> Active harming incidents have occurred at a number of locations in recent years, and the University of Colorado is not immune to this potential. While the odds of this occurring at CU are small, the consequences are so potentially catastrophic it makes sense for all students, staff, faculty and visitors to CU to consider the possibility of such an incident occurring here.

In making her argument against concealed-carry weapons to me, Levy painted a bit of a contradictory picture: On the one hand, campuses are the safest places in the country. On the other hand, campus life is so inherently dangerous that the introduction of even licensed guns could mean mayhem. "You're in this milieu of drugs and alcohol and impulsive behavior and mental illness; you've got a population that has a high propensity for suicide," she told me. "Theft is a big concern, and what if you had a concealed-carry gun and you're drinking and become violent?"...

Anti-gun advocates ... should acknowledge that gun-control legislation is not the only answer to gun violence.

A Balanced Approach to Gun Control

The ideology of gun-ownership absolutism doesn't appeal to me. Unlike hard-line gun-rights advocates, I do not believe that unregulated gun ownership is a defense against the rise of totalitarianism in America, because I do not think that America is ripe for totalitarianism. (Fear of a tyrannical, gun-seizing president is the reason many gun owners oppose firearms registration.)

But I am sympathetic to the idea of armed self-defense, because it does often work, because encouraging learned helplessness is morally corrupt, and because, however much I might wish it, the United States is not going to become Canada. Guns are with us, whether we like it or not. Maybe this is tragic, but it is also reality. So Americans who are qualified to possess firearms shouldn't be denied the right to participate in their own defense. And it is empirically true that the great majority of America's tens of millions of law-abiding gun owners have not created chaos in society.

A balanced approach to gun control in the United States would require the warring sides to agree on several contentious issues. Conservative gun-rights advocates should acknowledge that if more states had stringent universal background check—or if a federal law put these in place—more guns would be kept out of the hands of criminals and the dangerously mentally unstable. They should also acknowledge that requiring background checks on buyers at gun shows would not represent a threat to the Constitution. "The NRA position on this is a fiction," says Dan Gross, the head of the Brady Campaign. "Universal background checks are not an infringement on our Second Amendment rights. This is black-helicopter stuff." Gross believes that closing the gun-show loophole would be both extremely effective and a politically moderate and achievable goal. The gun lobby must also agree that concealed-carry permits should be granted only to people who pass rigorous criminal checks, as well as thorough training-and-safety courses.

Anti-gun advocates, meanwhile, should acknowledge that gun-control legislation is not the only answer to gun violence. Responsible gun ownership is also an answer. An enormous number of Americans believe this to be the case, and gun-control advocates do themselves no favors when they demonize gun owners, and advocates of armed self-defense, as backwoods barbarians. Liberals sometimes make the mistake of anthropomorphizing guns, ascribing to them moral characteristics they do not possess. Guns can be used to do evil, but guns can also be used to do good. Twelve years ago, in the aftermath of Matthew Shepard's murder [1998 in Wyoming], Jonathan Rauch launched a national movement when he wrote an article for *Salon* arguing that gay people should arm themselves against violent bigots. Pink Pistol clubs sprang up across America, in which gays and lesbians learn to use firearms in self-defense. Other vulnerable groups have also taken to the idea of concealed carry: in Texas, African American women represent the largest percentage increase of concealed-carry permit seekers since 2000.

But even some moderate gun-control activists, such as Dan Gross, have trouble accepting that guns in private hands can work effectively to counteract violence. When I asked him the question I posed to Stephen Barton [victim of shooting at Century 16 Cineplex in Aurora, Colorado in July 2012] and Tom Mausers—would you, at a moment when a stranger is shooting at you, prefer to have a gun, or not?—he answered by saying, "This is the conversation the gun lobby wants you to be having." He pointed out some of the obvious flaws in concealed-carry laws, such as too-lax training standards and too much discretionary power on the part of local law-enforcement officials. He did say that if concealed-carry laws required background checks and training similar to what police recruits undergo, he would be slower to raise objections. But then he added: "In a fundamental way, isn't this a question about the kind of society we want to live in?" Do we want to live in one "in which the answer to violence is more violence, where the answer to guns is more guns?"

What Gross won't acknowledge is that in a nation of nearly 300 million guns, his question is irrelevant.

9

Increased Civilian Gun Ownership Will Not Reduce Crime

Alex Seitz-Wald

Alex Seitz-Wald is a political correspondent for the National Journal.

The argument that arming more civilians will help save lives is flawed. Experts criticize the claim that armed civilians can prevent gun violence. Influential studies on the issue, purporting to support the argument that more guns lead to less crime, have been proven to be flawed. Guns owned by civilians are unlikely to be used effectively in a situation such as a mass shooting and, in fact, evidence points in the direction of more guns increasing the suicide and homicide rates.

By now, the response isn't even surprising. After a horrific massacre like the one in Newtown, Conn., last week [December 14, 2012], gun-rights advocates will argue that someone with a gun at the scene could have stopped the killer. They conclude that the answer to mass shootings is to arm more people.

The More Guns, Less Crime Argument

This argument is usually made by people who can be easily dismissed, like boffo U.S. Rep. Louie Gohmert, R-Texas, or Larry Pratt, the executive director of Gun Owners of America.

Pratt said this weekend that "gun control supporters have the blood of little children on their hands" for preventing law-abiding citizens from bringing guns into schools.

But the more guns/less crime argument shouldn't be dismissed so summarily. There's an undeniable intuitive logic to it—if you were facing down an active shooter, wouldn't you want to be armed? Nearly half of Americans keep a gun in their home—and the majority say the main reason they do so is to defend themselves. Across the country, states are expanding right to carry laws, which allow permitted citizens to carry concealed weapons for their own defense.

In this month's *Atlantic*, correspondent Jeffrey Goldberg set out to make the case in a smart and reasonable way that would be amenable to the kind of people who read the *Atlantic*. It's a fluke of timing that it hit newsstands just as Newtown reignited the gun debate. His massive 7,000-word feature, titled "The Case for More Guns (And More Gun Control)," makes a compelling argument in what could be called the "*Slate* pitch" genre of contrarian counternarratives that seek to provoke by challenging widely held, though rarely debated, assumptions. In this case, he questions whether more guns invariably lead to more gun violence.

Five of the country's most prominent researchers into gun violence . . . were uniformly critical of the "more guns" approach.

He advocates stricter gun restrictions like closing the gun show loophole and better training for people with concealed carry permits. But he concludes that with so many guns already in the hands of Americans (over 300 million, or about one per person) and the police incapable of protecting us, the situation is pretty much hopeless—so we're probably better off arming ourselves and other law-abiding citizens so we can defend ourselves.

Now, before we go any further, it's worth noting that Goldberg, in an email exchange, insisted, "I'm not advocating the addition of more guns into the population." When I pointed out the title of his essay is "The Case for More Guns," he explained, "I didn't write the headline." Sure, but the implication of Goldberg's argument is clear to anyone who reads it. He says he's arguing that people should be able to "participate in their own defense" and that armed law-abiding citizens can be a part of the solution. Either way, the end result is exactly the same: more guns.

Critics of the More-Guns Approach

When I reached out to five of the country's most prominent researchers into gun violence, they were uniformly critical of the "more guns" approach and Goldberg's argument for what they saw as an ignorance of the overwhelming body of social science research that shows unequivocally that more guns equals more deaths. Some used nasty words like "garbage" and "atrocious."

"My first impression is that this essay should be used as a case study for high school and college debate teams across the country. It is one of the best crafted arguments for a particular position I have ever read," said Arthur Kellermann, a prominent firearms safety researcher now at the RAND Corp. But he also called the research cited "highly selective, and therefore misleading." "I am surprised that the editors didn't ask their national correspondent why he didn't bother to talk to at least one mainstream criminologist, policy analyst, physician or public health researcher."

Fred Rivara, an epidemiologist at the University of Washington, added in an email: "There is no data supporting his argument that the further arming of citizens will lessen the death toll in massacres like the one this week in Connecticut.

There are in fact rigorous scientific data showing that having a gun in the home INCREASES the risk of violent death in the home."

Now, a huge problem when delving into gun safety research, as I wrote about in July [2012], is that Congress has suppressed, and in some cases explicitly outlawed, the use of government funds to research gun safety. Government funding is the largest source of basic scientific research like this, so the consequences of that decision are huge. Still, there is more than enough research out there to conclude beyond a reasonable doubt that more guns lead to more violence.

This *includes* people who have right-to-carry permits. Researchers at Johns Hopkins University recently conducted a review of all the existing academic literature on right-to-carry [RTC] and found: "The most consistent finding across studies which correct for these flaws is that RTC laws are associated with an increase in aggravated assaults." They estimated the increase to be about 1 to 9 percent, which may not sound like much—but with nearly 1 million aggravated assaults in the country every year, a small percentage change makes a big difference.

Researchers at Harvard have conducted numerous studies comparing data across states and countries with different gun laws and concluded, quite simply, "Where there are more guns, there is more homicide."

Daniel Webster, the director of the Johns Hopkins Center for Gun Policy and Research, explained in an interview: "It's hard to make the case, as some have done, that right-to-carry laws will lead to an enormous increase in violence. That does not appear to be the case. But it also does not appear to be the case that there is any beneficial effect."

"So if you want to argue that the reason we have so many mass shootings, the reason that the United States has a homicide rate about seven times higher than other developed countries, is because we don't allow enough concealed carry of firearms, the data just don't bear that out. And the thought experiment that you do is almost laughable," Webster added.

Colin Goddard, who became an advocate with the Brady Campaign after getting shot multiple times at the Virginia Tech shooting [April 16, 2007, in Blacksburg, Virginia], put it another way: "If more guns would lead to less crime, then why is America not the safest place in the world, with 300 million guns?"

Scholars sharply criticized [gun-rights advocate John Lott's] methodology for having "multiple very important flaws."

The Research of John Lott

Goldberg cites a number of studies that have become popular data points for gun-rights advocates. He also spoke with several academics of his own. One, whom he suggested I contact as well, is Adam Winkler of UCLA [University of California, Los Angeles]. He is a constitutional lawyer, not a scientist. The other is [economist] John Lott.

No one has done more to advance the "More Guns, Less Crime" argument than Lott (that was the title of his book), so telling his story is unavoidable. To be fair, Goldberg does not rely on Lott's research and mostly cites him as a pro-gun activist and commentator, a role he's taken up since falling into academic disrepute.

Working as an economist at Yale and the University of Chicago in the 1990s, Lott published a series of articles and a book that argued, for example, that more than 1,500 murders, 4,000 rapes and 60,000 aggravated assaults "would have been avoided yearly" if more states adopted right-to-carry laws. The research immediately entered the public discourse and that paper became one of the most downloaded in the history of the Social Science Research Network repository.

But other scholars sharply criticized his methodology for having "multiple very important flaws." For instance, he ignored the crack epidemic that ravaged urban, non-right-to-carry states but avoided rural, pro-gun states. ("This would never have been taken seriously if it had not been obscured by a maze of equations," Rutgers sociologist Ted Goertzel wrote). Meanwhile, New York Democratic Sen. Chuck Schumer suggested Lott was a gun industry lackey because his salary was funded by a foundation created by the owner of one of the country's largest gun makers.

But the real controversy started in 2000 when Lott was unable to produce any records of a national survey he claimed to have conducted. He said he lost the data in a computer crash, but was unable to produce any other records or the names of students who helped him with it, leading some critics to speculate that he fabricated the entire thing. Even conservative blogger Michelle Malkin eviscerated Lott over the data mystery.

Lott took another blow in 2003 when Julian Sanchez, a fellow at the libertarian CATO Institute (no fan of gun control), revealed that Mary Rosh, one of Lott's most vociferous public defenders on the Internet, was actually an alter ego created by Lott to boost his work and harangue critics. "In most circles, this goes down as fraud," Donald Kennedy, the then-editor of the prestigious journal *Science* wrote in an editorial. Lott is now a Fox News contributor.

In 2004, the National Academy of Sciences conducted a literature review that included Lott's work, and found "no credible evidence that the passage of right-to-carry laws decreases or increases violent crime."

The Results of a Survey

If Lott's work can be discarded, the other key evidence for the more guns, less crime camp comes from criminologists Gary Kleck and Marc Gertz, whose work in the 1990s argued that there are between 800,000 and 2.5 million defensive uses of guns in America every year. The number has been widely touted by gun-rights activists, but strongly criticized by other scholars.

Indeed, studies commissioned by the Department of Justice using different sets of more rigorous data put the number at 83,000 or 108,000, alternatively. In his essay, Goldberg quickly abandons the 2.5 million figure and seems to settle on the 108,000 level, which is 23 times lower than the Kleck-Gertz top number.

Harvard economist David Hemenway has been especially critical of Kleck-Gertz, pointing out "serious methodological deficiencies" in their numbers. The data came from a national telephone survey of 5,000 households, which found that about .6 percent said they had used guns to defend themselves in the past year. Assuming that proportion held true for all Americans households, they extrapolated from their sample to find the 2.5 million figure.

Guns are used to threaten and intimidate far more often than they are used in self-defense.

Beyond the mathematical issues with that approach, and sampling problems in their survey, Hemenway said the researchers were too credulous in believing respondents. For instance, he pointed to a poll that found that 6 percent of Americans said they had had personal contact with aliens. "The ABC News/*Washington Post* data on aliens are as good as or better," Hemenway quipped.

But perhaps the biggest problem with the Kleck-Gertz numbers is that one person's self-defense is another person's murder, as the case of George Zimmerman and Trayvon Martin [shooting occurred on February 26, 2012, in Sanford, Florida] demonstrated. Hemenway and a colleague conducted their own survey and then asked five criminal court judges to review their data to determine the legality of the incidents of defensive gun use reported by respondents. "A majority of the reported self-defense gun uses were rated as probably illegal by a majority of judges," they found.

The conclusion: "Guns are used to threaten and intimidate far more often than they are used in self-defense."

Kellermann said that citing Kleck and Gertz "while ignoring the work of [Philip J.] Cook, [Franklin] Zimring, [Richard] Rosenfeld, [J.] Ludwig, [L.W.] Sherman, [Garen J.] Wintemute, Hemenway, [Stephen] Teret, Webster, [Frederick P.] Rivara, Kellermann and others"—other gun researchers who had conflicting or newer data—is "intellectually dishonest."

The Problem of Mass Shootings

Then there's the question of looking at the gun issue through the lens of mass murders. Garen Wintemute, a public health researcher at the University of California, Davis, said in an interview that this leads to faulty conclusions. "Everybody is talking about how do we stop the next Sandy Hook [elementary school massacre in Newtown, Connecticut], but that's the totally wrong approach, because the next one will be totally different," he said.

More important, while mass shootings like the one in Newtown are always the catalyst for a debate over guns, they're a tiny fraction of the problem. There are about 20 mass shootings a year in this country, which altogether take the lives of perhaps several hundred people. But there were over 32,000 firearm-related deaths last year, the majority of which (almost 20,000) were suicides. There were also almost 850 accidental deaths from firearms. Among homicides, "far more common than mass killings are altercations where, because there is a gun available, someone ends up dead instead of a less lethal option," Wintemute said.

And this is the problem with focusing on how to stop mass killings: It ignores what happens when there isn't one.

"Let's say we flood the country with guns. We put guns in every school, every hospital—more guns everywhere. This kind of thing happens about 20 times a year in the United States; what are the chances that any one of those guns is ever going to be used to help prevent or abort a mass murder? Vanishingly small," Wintemute said.

"The problem is not the gun being there at that almost impossibly rare moment; it's what happens to that gun all the rest of the time," he said. With the introduction of the gun, regardless of its purpose, we can expect more violent deaths, Wintemute explained. We know, for instance, that the mere presence of a gun inside a house is associated with a nearly fivefold increased risk of suicide and threefold increased risk in homicide, according to a 2004 paper published by Centers for Disease Control researchers in the *American Journal of Epidemiology*. (That finding has been replicated in numerous studies.)

"Now, if there was somehow a way that we could make a gun magically appear when it was needed, and disappear otherwise, I think that's a good idea," Wintemute added with a laugh.

The Evidence on Armed Civilians

But let's look at armed civilians defending themselves in mass shooting situations, because this is perhaps the most emotionally compelling argument of the more guns, less crime camp.

There are certainly a number of cases in which an armed citizen stopped a mass murder, but they are few and far between. Very often in these cases, critics note, it is off-duty police officers and not average armed citizens who took action. Meanwhile, there are other cases in which an armed civilian proved *counterproductive*.

One case Goldberg cites is the shooting at Appalachian Law School [Grundy, Virginia] in 2002. In the Appalachian case, two off-duty police officers helped to subdue a shooter and ended up getting profiled in an NRA [National Rifle Association] magazine because of it. But it turns out the gunman was already out of ammunition and had dropped his firearm by the time they closed in on him with their weapons drawn. A police spokesman said that while the armed men were helpful, "the biggest heroes were [Ted] Besen and [Todd] Ross—the unarmed men who lunged at [the shooter]," the Kansas City Star reported.

It's kind of fantasy thinking to assume that armed citizens are going to take out the bad guy and that nothing will go wrong.

On the other hand, in the confusion after the shooting of former Rep. Gabrielle Giffords [January 8, 2011 in Tucson, Arizona], an armed citizen nearly shot the unarmed hero who had tackled alleged shooter Jared Loughner.

Often, guns are ineffective in these situations. At the mall shooting in Oregon earlier this month [December 2012], a right to carry permit holder was in the exact right place at the right time. He ducked behind a pillar, drew his handgun, and saw that the shooter was distracted as he tried to fix his rifle. But the man, 22-year-old Nick Meli, never pulled the trigger. "As I was going down to pull, I saw someone in the back of the Charlotte [store] move, and I knew if I fired and missed, I could hit them." he explained. After it was all over, he said he didn't regret his decision for a second.

Indeed, critics point out that civilians in an active-shooter environment might end up causing more harm than good by accidentally shooting innocent bystanders. "It's kind of fantasy thinking to assume that armed citizens are going to take out the bad guy and that nothing will go wrong," said Webster of Johns Hopkins.

Even police officers, who train endlessly for these kind of situations, make tragic mistakes all the time. In August [2012],

NYPD [New York City Police Department] officers shot all nine of the innocent bystanders who were injured during a standoff with a gunman at the Empire State Building. Overall, officers hit their target in only about one out of every five shots, Webster said.

The truth, as difficult as it is to accept, is that it's often impossible to stop a shooter no matter how many guns are present.

The truth is that it's extremely difficult for anyone, let alone a lightly trained and inexperienced civilian, to effectively respond to a shooter. The entire episode can take a matter of seconds and your body is fighting against you: Under extreme stress, reaction time slows, heart rate increases and fine motor skills deteriorate. Police train to build muscle memory that can overcome this reaction, but the training wears off after only a few months if not kept up.

In 2009, ABC's *20/20* demonstrated the problem with a clever experiment. They recruited a dozen or so students, gave them gun training that was more comprehensive than what most states require for concealed carry permits, and then entrusted them with a gun and told them they would have to fend off a shooter later that day. Separating them, they placed each one in a real classroom with other "students" (actually study compatriots). When a gunman burst in and started shooting, each student tried to respond by drawing his or her gun. Every single student failed, including several who had had years of practice shooting guns, and they all got shot (fortunately, it was just paintball bullets in real handguns).

The Claim That Guns Save Lives

The truth, as difficult as it is to accept, is that it's often impossible to stop a shooter no matter how many guns are present. John Hinckley Jr. [in March 1982] managed to nearly kill

[President] Ronald Reagan and permanently disable James Brady [press secretary] despite the fact that they were surrounded by dozens of heavily armed men with the best training imaginable. The only way to stop the incident would have been to prevent the offender from getting guns in the first place.

In an email exchange, Goldberg defended his essay and acknowledged the problem. "Of course the more guns there are, the more deaths you're going to have," he said. It's hard to square that admission with the rest of his argument, which favors expanding gun access. When I mentioned it to one of the researchers, he quipped that via the transitive property, Goldberg was arguing for more deaths.

But perhaps the biggest problem is the philosophy underpinning notions to arm more people. Goddard of the Brady campaign said it best in an interview: "The idea behind concealed carry is a kind of 'defend yourself and your family and f*** everybody else' mentality."

No serious person today is questioning the right of Americans to own guns, and without a doubt, you can find numerous cases in which guns have saved lives. But on balance, with the data available, it's close to impossible to make a convincing case that guns save lives. With 300 million guns already in circulation, it's hard to see a perfect solution, but encouraging more guns is certainly not the answer.

An unexpected bit of wisdom on this: Brad Dayspring, [US Congressman] Eric Cantor's former spokesman who now runs a GOP [Republican party] super PAC [political action committee], said on Twitter yesterday [December 2012], "The most effective way to avoid tragedies like this is not to start an arms race among teachers/students."

"America is not going to shoot our way out of the gun violence problem, and that's what these people are calling for. And I think that's dangerous and I think that will lead to more of us being killed by bullets," Goddard said.

10

Face It: Guns Are Here to Stay

Trevor Burrus

Trevor Burrus is a research fellow at the Cato Institute's Center for Constitutional Studies.

It must be accepted that guns will never be eliminated from the United States and that the best gun policies are those that accept this fact. Rather than trying to remove guns from law-abiding citizens, gun-control advocates should recognize that there are many instances where law-abiding gun owners help to prevent crime or stop it altogether. States that allow concealed-carry guns have not seen an increase in crime, but those carrying guns have been able to use their weapons in self-defense.

The horrific massacre in Newtown, Conn., is reigniting the debate over guns—which must begin with the realistic premise that there will never be a gun-free America. Until we own up to this truth, we won't get anywhere.

An emotional revulsion toward guns inhibits productive dialogue between gun-control advocates and their opponents. For many gun-control supporters, a good world is one where private ownership of guns is both unnecessary and illegal.

I have sympathy for the appeal of this ideal, but such a daydream cannot guide our public policy.

There are approximately 300 million guns in private hands in the United States. Even if the government enacted a massive program to confiscate these weapons, the feds would fail in their task and frighten millions of Americans in the process.

And if they did somehow manage to take away legal weapons? That would still leave criminals happily armed.

We must simply accept the inevitability of an America teeming with guns (to the chagrin of Piers Morgan and his fellow liberals). If we at least agree on this realistic starting point, we can move the debate toward reasonable and effective policy proposals: better mental-health care to prevent seriously ill people with violent tendencies from acquiring weapons; background checks; better enforcement of existing laws.

None of these need to involve taking guns out of the hands of law-abiding Americans in order for us to avoid the next Newtown. In fact, guns may well help prevent it.

In December 2007, for example, Matthew Murray entered the New Life Church in Colorado Springs, Colo., armed with two handguns and an assault rifle (the same arsenal possessed by Adam Lanza). Murray had killed two people in the parking lot before entering the church. Inside, he shot one man in the arm before being shot by Jeanne Assam, a former police officer with a concealed-carry permit.

Potential massacres were also stopped in 1997 at a Pearl, Miss., school and in 1998 at a school dance in Edinboro, Pa. In both cases, responsible citizens prevented mass bloodshed by drawing their weapons and using them for the public good. Mock the NRA's Wayne LaPierre all you want, but in those two cases—and plenty of others—good guys with a gun did save the day.

Forty-one states currently have safe and effective concealed-carry permitting systems, and eight other states have more restrictive discretionary permitting laws. Since the 1980s, there has been a profusion of states that allow concealed carry and—despite the dire predictions of many—there has been no corresponding increase in crime rates.

Permit holders are not having parking-lot shootouts or brandishing their weapons during mall scrums over toys. In the past 20 years, the cases of permit holders using their guns improperly are quite rare—and they are certainly much rarer than the times in which people used a concealed weapon to successfully defend themselves.

In short, we have become a society that allows widespread gun-carrying for law-abiding citizens, and this has occurred largely in silence not because of political pressure by the gun lobby or cowardice by Democrats but because there is almost nothing to report.

Almost nothing. We have been mostly silent about just how many times Americans use guns to lawfully and successfully defend themselves from crime.

At minimum, according to the Justice Department's own data, this occurs about 110,000 times per year.

There are, however, many reasons to suspect that this data severely under-reports the true number; other studies have found that Americans use guns defensively between 830,000 and 2.45 million times per year.

Moreover, these numbers don't include the inherently immeasurable instances where would-be criminals decided not to commit a specific crime due to the fear that the would-be victim might be carrying a gun.

In the wake of the Newtown tragedy, stricter gun laws will almost certainly be proposed. But if we make the reasonable assumption that criminals will evade these laws if at all possible, and that identifying shooters before their crimes is a monumentally difficult task, then we can start to deal with actually attainable, second-best solutions.

While we should do everything we can to prevent massacres like Newtown, we should also remember what it takes to stop a New Life Church.

11

Treasure the Second Amendment, but Ban Assault Rifles

Judith Miller

Judith Miller is a writer for Newsmax.

After the 2012 mass shooting inside a movie theater in Aurora, Colorado, it is time for politicians to do something. The Second Amendment to the US Constitution gives American citizens the right to own guns, but it does not give them the right to own assault weapons. The Federal Assault Weapons Ban of 1994 should be reinstated, banning the manufacture and sale of certain semi-automatic firearms and magazines.

I have a dream to counter the nightmare of Aurora. I see three or four ex-presidents standing together, speaking truth to the American people. Here is what they would say: "Our fellow Americans, we have come together not as Democrats or Republicans, but as men who have been privileged to lead this great country.

"We all treasure the constitution and the Second Amendment. We believe that Americans have the right to own guns. But that amendment does not entitle citizens to own combat weapons like the assault weapon that the Aurora shooter used to kill 12 and wound 58 more in a Colorado theater.

"The AR-15 assault rifle is a military-style weapon designed to feature high-capacity ammunition magazines capable of firing up to 30 rounds of ammunition without re-loading. You don't need an assault weapon to protect your family or shoot a deer. No one should own an assault rifle except our folks in the military and the law enforcement officers who protect us.

"For 10 years, assault weapons like these were banned in all 50 states until Congress let the Federal Assault Weapons Ban 'sunset.'

"Our fellow Americans, it's time to reinstate this law. We call upon the men who lead, or want to lead this country, and the Congress, to do the right thing: Protect American citizens by restricting the sale of such weapons to those who have been authorized to use them."

Is such a group presidential statement a pipe dream?

Former President Jimmy Carter has long called for reinstating the assault weapons ban. So, too, did President Clinton.

Can't we do more than pray for families of victims and carry flowers to their graves?

In 1994 Clinton signed two bills that became the hallmark of such efforts. The Brady Handgun Violence Protection Act required a five-day waiting period and background check for the sale of handguns and created a National Instant Criminal Background Check System.

The Assault Weapons bill he signed banned the production and importing of 19 types of military-style semiautomatic assault weapons and other guns with similar features, as well as ammunition magazines containing more than 10 rounds.

Sen. Dianne Feinstein remains in the Senate. She led the campaign for the ban after a series of shootings in her state of California, including a 1993 rampage in a San Francisco office building that left eight dead and six wounded.

She could help lead the charge in the Senate. And Rep. Carolyn McCarthy, of Long Island, has never stopped trying to ban high-capacity ammunition clips, like the one used to kill 6 people and wound 14, including Rep. Gabby Giffords, in yet another Wild West rampage.

McCarthy's own husband was gunned down and her son seriously injured in a shooting in 1993 on a Long Island commuter train.

President George H.W. Bush signed an executive order making it illegal to import Uzis and AK-47s. Even his son, President George W. Bush, whose opposition to gun control may have helped him eke out victory over Al Gore, indicated in 2004 that he would have signed an assault weapons ban reauthorization had Congress approved it.

If not now, when? How many more massacres must Americans endure—the assassination of John F. Kennedy, the tragedy of Columbine, the Amish girls killings, the Virginia Tech murders, the Fort Hood tragedy, the Gabby Giffords shootings? Can't we do more than pray for families of victims and carry flowers to their graves?

I believe that most Americans would welcome a call-to-arms against combat arms protection from our former presidents.

I think that many have yearned to hear a speech like that from President Obama and Mitt Romney, his would-be replacement. But neither had the guts to mention the "g" word.

Instead, they stopped campaigning for two whole days and spoke of the "horrific and tragic" massacre and of coming together as "one American family" to pray and grieve about the "senseless violence," as if we had just suffered a tsunami rather than a historic failure of political courage.

It was pathetic.

Only New York's Mayor Mike Bloomberg called upon Obama and Romney to join him in restricting such weapons. "Soothing words are nice," he said, "but maybe it's time that the two people who want to be president of the United States stand up and tell us what they are going to do about it."

Amen.

OK. Guns don't kill people. But in Aurora, the undoubtedly unhinged person who struck had four of them—an assault rifle, as well as a Remington 12-gauge shotgun, and two .40 caliber Glock handguns.

In the last 60 days, police said, he bought more than 6,000 rounds of ammunition: more than 3,000 rounds for the assault rifle, 3,000 rounds of .40 caliber ammunition for the two Glocks, and 300 rounds for the 12-gauge shotgun—all on the Internet.

When is enough enough? When will our politicians be moral and principled enough to do more than utter empty platitudes and challenge the gun lobby on what should be a no-brainer?

12

A Ban on Assault Weapons Would Not Reduce Crime

National Rifle Association Institute for Legislative Action (NRA-ILA)

The National Rifle Association Institute for Legislative Action (NRA-ILA) is the lobbying arm of the National Rifle Association (NRA).

Bans on assault weapons and large ammunition magazines are misguided and conflict with the guarantee of the Second Amendment. So-called assault weapons—semi-automatic firearms—are different than military weapons and not necessarily more powerful than other guns. Furthermore, the existence of such weapons does not correlate with more violent crime. Past assault weapons bans show that these laws do not reduce crime and criminals find ways around them.

Introduction: In the late 1980s, gun control groups realized that they had failed in their original goal—getting handguns banned—and began campaigning against semi-automatic firearms they called "assault weapons," most of which are rifles. As an anti-gun activist [Violence Policy Center] group put it:

> [A]ssault weapons [will] strengthen the handgun restriction lobby for the following reasons: It will be a new topic in what has become to the press and public an "old" debate

... [H]andgun restriction consistently remains a non-issue with the vast majority of legislators, the press, and public ... Efforts to restrict assault weapons are more likely to succeed than those to restrict handguns ... Although the opportunity to restrict assault weapons exists, a question remains for the handgun restriction movement: "How?"

Most guns that are traced have not been used to commit violent crimes, and most guns used to commit violent crimes are never traced.

Reasons to Reject Firearm Bans

Gun control supporters demanding a ban on "assault weapons" have also demanded a ban on ammunition magazines that hold more than 10 rounds, most of which are designed for self-defense handguns. These gun and magazine bans should be rejected because:

Reason #1: Semi-automatic firearms are not fully-automatic military machine guns. Gun control supporters say that *semi*-automatic rifles like the AR-15 are "military-style assault weapons" designed for "war" on "the battlefield." To the contrary, the military uses *fully*-automatic rifles, which are regulated as "machineguns" by the National Firearms Act of 1934. The difference is that a fully-automatic firearm can fire repeatedly and quickly as long as you hold down the trigger, but a semi-automatic, like any firearm other than a fully-automatic, fires only once when you pull the trigger.

Reason #2: Semi-automatic firearms are not "more powerful" than other guns. Gun control supporters call "assault weapons" (and all other firearms, for that matter) "high-powered." However, a firearm's power is determined by the caliber or gauge of its ammunition; semi-automatic rifles and shotguns use the same ammunition as many other rifles and shotguns, and semi-automatic handguns use ammunition comparable to revolver ammunition. So-called "assault weapons" are much less powerful than many rifles used to hunt deer and other large game.

Reason #3: As the numbers of "assault weapons" and "large" magazines have soared to all-time highs, violent crime has been cut in half. The nation's total violent crime rate peaked in 1991. Since then, through 2012, it has decreased 49%, to a 42-year low, including a 52% drop in the nation's murder rate, to a 49-year low—perhaps the lowest point in American history. Meanwhile, the number of the most popular firearm that gun control supporters call an "assault weapon"—the AR-15 semi-automatic rifle—has risen by over 4.5 million, the number of all semi-automatic firearms has risen by over 50 million, and the total number of privately-owned firearms has risen by over 130 million. The number of new magazines that hold more than 10 rounds has risen by many tens of millions.

Reason #4: So-called "assault weapons" have never been used in more than a small percentage of firearm-related violent crime. The study that Congress required of the federal "assault weapon" and "large" magazine ban of 1994–2004 concluded that "the banned weapons and magazines were never used in more than a modest fraction of all gun murders" even before the ban, and that the law's 10-round limit on new ammunition magazines wasn't a factor in multiple-victim or multiple-wound crimes. A follow-up study [by D.C. Reedy and C.S. Koper] found "gunshot injury incidents involving pistols (which use magazines) were less likely to produce a death than were those involving revolvers" (which don't use magazines), and "the average number of wounds for pistol victims was actually lower than that for revolver victims." Police reports and felon surveys have found that "assault weapons" are used in only 1%-2% of violent crimes. The vast majority of firearms that gun control supporters call "assault weapons" are rifles, and during the most recent five years of data, there were nine times as many murders with knives, blunt objects (hammers, clubs, etc.), and "personal weapons" (hands, feet, etc.), as with rifles of any type.

Reason #5: "Assault weapon" and "large" magazine bans have not reduced crime. After its 1989 ban, California's murder rate increased every year for five years, 26% overall. California banned more guns in January 2000 (and thereafter imposed a variety of other gun control restrictions) and murder has since averaged 12% higher than the national rate. The Bureau of Alcohol, Tobacco, Firearms and Explosives [BATFE] says it can "in no way vouch for the validity" of Brady Campaign's claim—repeated by "assault weapon" ban campaigner Sen. Diane Feinstein (D-Calif.)—that the federal "assault weapon" law reduced crime. (Brady [Campaign to Prevent Gun Violence] mischaracterized BATFE's firearm chain-of-commerce traces, which the Congressional Research Service says "are not accurate indicators" of criminal gun use. Most guns that are traced have *not* been used to commit violent crimes, and most guns used to commit violent crimes are never traced.) Even the radical anti-gun group, Violence Policy Center, said "You can't argue with a straight face that the ban has been effective." The FBI [Federal Bureau of Investigation] does not list guns or "gun control" as a "crime factor" and California doesn't credit its "assault weapon" ban for the state's recent decrease in crime. Studies for the CDC [US Centers for Disease Control and Prevention], the National Academy of Sciences, and the Library of Congress have found no evidence that "gun control" reduces crime.

Reason #6: Criminals could easily get around a limit on newly-manufactured magazines. As noted, Americans already own tens of millions of magazines that hold more than 10 rounds. If the manufacture of new such magazines were banned, the cost of pre-ban magazines would rise (as it did when the 1994 ban was imposed), but any criminal determined to have them would always be able to get them, including by theft from law-abiding owners. A criminal could carry multiple limited-capacity magazines and use them to reload a firearm quickly. The official report on the worst mass shooting in American history concluded that a limit on magazine capacity would not have changed the outcome of that crime. A criminal could also carry multiple guns. A criminal could also resort to a method other than a firearm.

Handguns are the most popular weapon chosen by Americans *for self-defense in the home.*

Reason #7: Criminals could switch to more concealable guns. When the federal "large" magazine ban of 1994–2004 was imposed, limiting the capacity of new magazines to 10 rounds, many gun owners switched from full-size handguns holding between 13–17 rounds, to small "sub-compact" models holding only 10 rounds. This is ironic, because the firearms that gun control supporters most wanted to see banned from the 1970s until they refocused their energies on "assault weapons," were compact handguns, which (as a thinly veiled insult to the African-American community) they called "Saturday Night Specials."

Reason #8: Criminals could switch to more powerful guns. Another response to the 1994 federal law limiting new magazines to 10 rounds was the switch by many gun owners to handguns which, instead of holding between 13–17 rounds of small-caliber handgun ammunition, held exactly 10 rounds of large-caliber handgun ammunition. As with the sub-compact 10-round models mentioned above, such handguns are now commonplace.

Reason #9: The Second Amendment protects the right to semi-automatic firearms and magazines designed for self-defense. In *District of Columbia v. Heller* (2008), the first case ever in which the Supreme Court was asked to rule on whether the Second Amendment protects an individual right to keep and bear arms for defensive purposes, the court ruled that historically "the inherent right of self-defense has been central to the Second Amendment right" and that the amendment guarantees "the individual right to possess and carry weapons in case of confrontation." At issue in *Heller* was the District's bans on handguns and on having other firearms assembled and loaded for protection within the home. The court declared both bans unconstitutional, saying "handguns are the most popular weapon *chosen by Americans* for self-defense in the home."

Gun control supporters had argued that the Founding Fathers could not have envisioned semi-automatic firearms, and thus the Second Amendment protected the right to own only 18th century firearms such as muskets. However, the court dismissed that notion, saying "some have made the argument, bordering on the frivolous, that only those arms in existence in the 18th century are protected by the Second Amendment. We do not interpret constitutional rights that way. Just as the First Amendment protects modern forms of communication and the Fourth Amendment applies to modern forms of search, the Second Amendment extends, prima facie, to all instruments that constitute bearable arms, even those that were not in existence at the time of the founding."

Based upon a disputable interpretation of the court's decision in *U.S. v. Miller* (1939), the *Heller* court commented, in dicta, that it believed that fully-automatic firearms could be banned, on the grounds that they are not "in common use." (Justice Stephen Breyer noted in his otherwise flawed dissent in *Heller* that fully-automatic firearms are not "in common use" only because they have been heavily restricted under federal and state laws. One might also note that fully-automatic firearms are, in fact, "in common use" among the organized component of the Militia of the United States, the National Guard; the federal and state restrictions mentioned apply only to the unorganized component of the Militia, able-bodied males of age who are not part of the organized Militia or of the Armed Forces of the United States.)

The *Heller* court did not address semi-automatic firearms. Semi-automatics were introduced in the late 1800s, and today account for over 15 percent of all privately owned firearms in the United States. The AR-15, a semi-automatic rifle that gun control supporters call an "assault weapon," is the most popular rifle on the market today. The landmark [researchers Gary] Kleck-[Marc] Gertz survey of defensive firearms uses found that 40% of all such uses are performed with semi-automatic handguns. All firearms used in the annual National Rifle and Pistol Trophy Matches are semi-automatic.

While a police officer can carry extra magazines on his duty belt, *and* have a rifle or shotgun in his patrol car, *and* call for back-up, a private citizen attacked in a parking lot, or at home in the middle of the night, will probably have only the magazine within the firearm. No one should be arbitrarily limited in the number of rounds he or she can have for self-defense.

Reason #10: The slippery slope. Gun control supporters have attempted to apply the "assault weapon" label to more and more semi-automatic firearms and, in some instances, even to pump-action firearms. California expanded its 1989 "assault weapon" ban in 2000. The 1989 ban's sponsor in the state assembly said that the 1989 ban "did what we wanted to do. We got our nose under the tent. We saw this as a beginning." As the federal "assault weapon" ban of 1994 was about to expire, a bill was introduced in Congress to dramatically expand the number of firearms it banned, including all semi-automatic shotguns, the historic M1 Garand, and the M1 carbine. In 1993, Sen. Dianne Feinstein (D-Calif.) introduced the federal "assault weapon" ban, applying to 19 firearms by name; her 2013 bill proposed to ban 120. Some magazine limits have been arbitrarily set at 10 or as few as seven rounds, but limits of six and even three rounds have been suggested.

13

There Is No Easy Solution to Preventing Gun Violence

Richard A. Epstein

Richard A. Epstein is the Peter and Kirsten Bedford Senior Fellow at the Hoover Institution and the Laurence A. Tisch Professor of Law at New York University School of Law.

There are many pitfalls to implementing effective sanctions to deter or punish gun crime and implementing fair and effective gun-control measures. Mass shooters are not often responsive to the threat of punishment, especially if suicide is already part of their plan. Gun-control measures are often overbroad, preventing law-abiding citizens from attaining guns. Furthermore, there is a risk of shifting gun ownership completely to criminals. These pitfalls must be kept in mind when enacting measures intended to stop gun violence.

Once more, America gropes for a magic bullet.

The macabre tragedy in Aurora, Colorado [July 20, 2012], which left at least 12 people dead and 58 seriously wounded, is a grim reminder of the helpless position in which innocent people can find themselves at the hands of a maniac. No fictional film can top the tale of James Holmes, a former graduate student in neuroscience, who was decked out in "ballistic" regalia as he entered the Century 16 movie theater shortly after midnight during a showing of *The Dark Knight Rises*.

Armed with assault weapons and tear or smoke gas bombs, he first immobilized and then shot his victims without reason or remorse. To top matters off, he then booby-trapped his apartment in an apparent effort to kill or maim the police officers that were likely to search it.

It is easy to condemn Holmes's dastardly actions. It is harder to figure out what to do now. No one should make light of the difficulties involved in trying to craft a sensible policy in response to such senseless behavior. But the sad truth is that there is precious little that any society can do to defend itself against these periodic tragedies that crop up every several years or so.

The Challenges with Sanctions

To see why, it is necessary to adopt a clinical, detached, and cautious attitude, which seems so utterly ill-suited for the occasion. That analytical approach divides the inquiry into two parts. The first asks about the sanctions that can be directed against the individual miscreant who committed the particular actions. The second asks about the institutional responses that could be enacted to nip such tragedies in the bud. Both face many pitfalls on the path toward implementation.

The assumption of rational behavior often does not hold in dealing with mass murderers.

In dealing with individual criminals, every legal system imposes punishments on particular actions once the wrong-doer has been caught. There is a long-standing disagreement as to the proper grounds for this punishment. Some argue that it is a form of retribution for the wrong done, which society imposes to express its eternal distaste for the conduct in question. Others regard that position as a form of posturing and think that the proper justification for the use of criminal sanctions, including capital punishment, is to deter other individuals from performing similar actions.

In many ways, the debate between the two sides is overwrought, because there is a high level of operational agreement between the two sides on the proper principles for governing that punishment. The common view is to make the punishment fit the crime so that, roughly speaking, the more serious the offense, the harsher the punishment in question.

Neither the theory of deterrence nor the theory of retribution works for persons who choose to take their own lives.

In working with the criminal justice system, the deterrence theory has, on balance, won out if only because its instrumental approach seems to offer clear guidelines for the use of public force. But the economic analysis that drives modern punishment theory also explains why any social response to mass murder is likely to fall short. The first difficulty arises in connection with the theory of proportionality, which implies that the more severe the crime is, then the more severe the punishment should be. Unfortunately, this approach cannot be strictly applied so long as death sets an upper bound on punishment. That difficulty is even more acute in places like Norway, where Anders Breivik, the self-confessed murderer of 77 people, faces a maximum sentence of 21 years in prison for a crime that everyone knows he committed. The sad truth is that there is systematic under-deterrence for the most severe crimes, which is offset only partially by the proper social willingness to criminalize attempted murder and other activities, like conspiracy and aiding and abetting, that deserve state punishment even in the absence of actual harm.

The Faulty Assumption of Rational Behavior

Another problem is that the assumption of rational behavior often does not hold in dealing with mass murderers. The usual model of economic behavior postulates *normal*—I use this word consciously—individuals who respond to incentives. The higher the price, either in cash or personal inconvenience, that they have to pay for a given activity, the less likely they are to engage in it. This basic model, which explains why people decrease their purchase of a good whose price has increased, can also explain why people are less likely to engage in criminal behavior when the legal sanctions increase.

This model may work well with hired killers and bank robbers, but it often does not hold with weird people who, on a single occasion, choose to commit mass murders. Both Holmes and Breivik are unusual in that they were captured alive after committing their atrocities. Mass killers often commit suicide after wreaking mayhem or put up fierce resistance so that law enforcement officers will kill them.

The gunman who took the lives of 32 people at Virginia Tech [Blacksburg, Virginia] in 2007 committed suicide after the event; the same is true with the two students who killed 13 people and wounded over 20 more in Columbine [High School in Littleton, Colorado, in 1999]. This often happens on a smaller scale: It is estimated that about one-third of distraught men who kill women commit suicide afterward. Neither the theory of deterrence nor the theory of retribution works for persons who choose to take their own lives.

The Effectiveness of Gun Control Laws

Given the systemic weaknesses of individual deterrence, is there a set of sanctions and regulations that can be implemented *before* these pathological maniacs can wreak harm on other individuals? This is the question that every serious analyst must ask. The most common response demands the imposition of some form of gun control laws that can take weapons out of the hands of miscreants, both rational and irrational, before they can do any harm.

As I have already argued ..., we can put aside any misguided claims that the Second Amendment offers special protection to gun holders. The harder question is whether gun control laws actually do any good. The issue here involves both the choice of social ends, and the means to achieve them. Gun control laws score high on the first point: Protection against armed violence is, even in the most libertarian of states, a legitimate social objective. The control of force includes elimination of the threat of the use of force as well.

Today, upwards of 200 million firearms of all descriptions are available for general use in the United States.

All of the action, however, lies on the second point, which asks whether the means chosen (gun control) advance the end in question (fewer murders). For many people, like New York's Mayor Michael Bloomberg, the answer to this question rises to an article of faith:

> You know, to arm everybody and have the Wild West all the time is one of the more nonsensical things you can say.... The bottom line is if we had fewer guns, we would have a lot fewer murders.

Unfortunately the underlying reality is a lot more complicated than Bloomberg's simplistic syllogism suggests. It is always hard to design licensing systems to stop dangerous behaviors like driving automobiles, controlling the sale of hard drugs, or using guns. The root of the problem is this: The *ex post* remedy that goes after wrongdoers runs only a small risk of over-breadth, which can usually be limited by having suitable punishment procedures. Licensing regimes, in contrast, are always overbroad. They will result in social losses by stopping the use of guns, cars, or drugs (think medical marijuana) by people who will make perfectly legitimate use of the dangerous instrument in question.

Perhaps those like Mayor Bloomberg will respond that these losses are a small price to pay for the prevention of unnecessary deaths. But even that generalization may turn out to be false, as the bad actors whom the licensing system targets are the most willing to circumvent that system. The selective enforcement of these tough prohibitions could easily cause more harm than good: Think of the black market trade in drugs fostered by the war on drugs.

This same dynamic *could* be at work in dealing with guns. Today, upwards of 200 million firearms of all descriptions are available for general use in the United States. Amnesty programs have made only a tiny dent in that number. The imposition of a tough registration program will lead to a substantial reduction in the number of guns in circulation. But even tough gun laws may have had little impact on people like James Holmes. Holmes showed no danger signs, except perhaps that he was a bit of a loner, not an uncommon trait. He had cleared all background checks when he purchased his weapon. If Colorado banned guns, would he have acquired the same weapons out of state or in the illegal market? No one knows.

The Unintended Consequences of Gun Control

The situation is even more complex when the focus shifts to the impact of gun laws more generally. Here, the key insight is that reducing the total number of guns is not the only likely effect of the law. The prohibitions in question will also shift the ratio of guns held in lawful and unlawful hands to favor the latter. To take the extreme case, suppose that a gun control law can eliminate 99.9 percent of the guns now in circulation and that all of the remaining 200,000 guns are in the hands of hardened criminals. We can confidently predict that crime will go up unless and until there is a vast expansion of the public police force.

Less dramatic shifts in that critical ratio should produce less dramatic results, but ones that cut in the same direction. Potential criminals, knowing that they are less likely to meet armed resistance will, on average, be more likely to commit various kinds [of] offenses. The empirical data suggests that this grim logic might even apply to mass killers intent on suicide, who do not like the prospect of being gunned down by strangers before they can kill their desired targets.

Indeed, at least one serious academic paper by the economists John Lott and William Landes finds a positive connection between tough gun laws and an increase in mass killings. That data could easily be disputed. But what cannot be denied is the intelligible economic theory that undergirds its conclusions. The basic point here is that in any gun-free environment (such as that of Virginia Tech), the assailant knows that he will not meet with any immediate armed resistance, and this puts innocent people at risk.

So what then to do? It may well be that the best strategy is a combination of both carrots and sticks. A ban on the sale and possession of assault weapons makes sense on the ground if it is true that there are few lawful uses of guns and many dangerous ones. One does not have to lurch to Mayor Bloomberg's intemperate Wild-West scenario to think that it may well be wise to increase the use of concealed firearms by off-duty police officers, military people, and private security guards who normally carry these weapons as part of their jobs. The task of preventing violence requires a difficult balancing act that is inconsistent with both a fierce defense and a fierce denunciation of all gun control measures.

Organizations to Contact

The editors have compiled the following list of organizations concerned with the issues debated in this book. The descriptions are derived from materials provided by the organizations. All have publications or information available for interested readers. The list was compiled on the date of publication of the present volume; names, addresses, phone and fax numbers, and e-mail and Internet addresses may change. Be aware that many organizations take several weeks or longer to respond to inquiries, so allow as much time as possible.

Brady Campaign to Prevent Gun Violence
1225 Eye St. NW, Suite 1100, Washington, DC   20005
(202) 898-0792
website: www.bradycampaign.org

The Brady Campaign to Prevent Gun Violence is part of the Brady organization, a nonprofit, nonpartisan organization working to make it harder for convicted felons, the dangerously mentally ill, and others like them to get guns. Through the Brady Campaign to Prevent Gun Violence, its network of Million Mom March chapters, and the Brady Center to Prevent Handgun Violence, the organization rallies for sensible gun laws, regulations, and public policies and works to educate the public about gun violence. Available at its website are numerous fact sheets, studies, and reports about gun control regulations, gun trafficking, public opinion, and other issues.

Cato Institute
1000 Massachusetts Ave. NW, Washington, DC   20001
(202) 842-0200 • fax: (202) 842-3490
website: www.cato.org

The Cato Institute is a public policy research organization dedicated to the principles of individual liberty, limited government, free markets, and peace. The Cato Institute is dedicated to increasing and enhancing the understanding of key public policies and to realistically analyzing their impact on the principles identified above. The Institute publishes many publications, such as the quarterly *Regulation* magazine, the bimonthly *Cato Policy Report*, and the periodic *Cato Journal*, and its website includes numerous articles, blogs, and studies dealing with the issue of gun ownership and regulation.

Children's Defense Fund (CDF)

25 E St. NW, Washington, DC   20001
(800) 233-1200
e-mail: cdfinfo@childrensdefense.org
website: www.childrensdefense.org

The Children's Defense Fund (CDF) is a nonprofit child advocacy organization that works to ensure a level playing field for all American children. CDF's Protect Children Not Guns campaign aims to protect children instead of guns. CDF publishes the annual *Protect Children Not Guns* report, which is available at its website.

Coalition to Stop Gun Violence (CSGV)

805 15th St. NW, Suite 700, Washington, DC   20005
(202) 408-0061
e-mail: csgv@csgv.org
website: www.csgv.org

The Coalition to Stop Gun Violence (CSGV) is comprised of forty-seven national organizations working to reduce gun violence. CSGV seeks to secure freedom from gun violence through aggressive political advocacy and research. CSGV has links on its website to the reports, memos, testimony, and websites of its member organizations.

Everytown for Gun Safety

e-mail: info@everytown.org
website: www.everytown.org

Everytown for Gun Safety is a movement of Americans working toward policies that will reduce gun violence. Everytown was formed by combining the Mayors Against Illegal Guns effort, founded in 2006 by former New York City mayor Michael Bloomberg and former Boston mayor Tom Menino, and Moms Demand Action for Gun Sense in America, a grassroots movement of US mothers that was founded on the day following the massacre at Sandy Hook Elementary in Newtown, Connecticut, in December 2012. Everytown is the largest gun violence prevention organization in the country with more than one and a half million supporters. Its efforts include supporting leaders and laws that promote gun safety, restricting child access to guns, and addressing gun violence in areas such as guns on campus, domestic violence, and suicide. Reports, videos, and fact sheets are available at its website.

Jews for the Preservation of Firearms Ownership (JPFO)
PO Box 270143, Hartford, WI   53027
(262) 673-9745 • fax: (262) 673-9746
e-mail: jpfo@jpfo.org
website: www.jpfo.org

Jews for the Preservation of Firearms Ownership (JPFO) is a nonprofit organization with the goal of opposing and reversing gun-control laws. JPFO works to educate the public on the danger of disarmament policies, and the organization has produced several films on the issue of gun control, including *Innocents Betrayed* and *2A Today for the USA*. It also publishes information on gun ownership that is available at its website.

National Firearms Association (NFA)
PO Box 49090, Edmonton, Alberta   T6E 6H4
  Canada
(877) 818-0393 • fax: (780) 439-4091
e-mail: info@nfa.ca
website: www.nfa.ca

The National Firearms Association (NFA) works for and with Canadian gun owners. The NFA supports legislation that reflects the needs of Canadian gun owners. The NFA publishes the *Canadian Firearms Journal*.

National Institute of Justice (NIJ)

810 Seventh St. NW, Washington, DC   20531
(800) 851-3420
website: www.nij.gov

The National Institute of Justice (NIJ) is the research, development, and evaluation agency of the US Department of Justice,
dedicated to improving knowledge and understanding of
crime and justice issues through science. NIJ provides objective and independent knowledge and tools to reduce crime
and promote justice, particularly at the state and local levels.
NIJ provides data, graphs, and reports about gun violence,
which is available at its website.

National Rifle Association (NRA)

11250 Waples Mill Rd., Fairfax, VA   22030
(800) 672-3888
website: www.nra.org

The National Rifle Association (NRA) is America's largest organization of gun owners and a powerful pro-gun rights
group. The NRA's Institute for Legislative Action lobbies
against restrictive gun-control legislation. In addition to fact
sheets published by its Institute for Legislative Action, the
NRA publishes the journals *American Rifleman, American
Hunter,* and *America's 1st Freedom.*

Second Amendment Committee

PO Box 1776, Hanford, CA   93232
(559) 584-5209 • fax: (559) 584-4084
e-mail: liberty89@libertygunrights.com
website: www.libertygunrights.com

The Second Amendment Committee, founded by a longtime
gun-rights activist, is a nationwide organization that aims to
protect the right to keep and bear arms. The Second Amendment Committee has authored pro-gun legislation, works to
ensure full protection of the right to bear arms, and speaks

out in support of citizen militias in the United States. The Second Amendment Committee has a variety of relevant documents available at its website.

Second Amendment Foundation (SAF)
12500 NE 10th Place, Bellevue, WA   98005
(800) 426-4302 • fax: (425) 451-3959
website: www.saf.org

The Second Amendment Foundation (SAF) is dedicated to promoting a better understanding of the constitutional heritage to privately own and possess firearms. SAF develops educational and legal action programs designed to better inform the public about the gun control debate. SAF publishes the *Journal on Firearms & Public Policy* and *Women & Guns*.

Stop Handgun Violence (SHV)
One Bridge St., Suite 300, Newton, MA   02458
(617) 243-8124 • fax: (617) 965-7308
e-mail: shv@stophandgunviolence.com
website: www.stophandgunviolence.com

Stop Handgun Violence (SHV) is a nonprofit organization committed to the prevention of gun violence through public awareness and legislation, without banning guns. SHV aims to increase public awareness about gun violence through media and public education campaigns. Available at its website are gun violence facts, stories, and information about its media campaigns.

Violence Policy Center (VPC)
1730 Rhode Island Ave. NW, Suite 1014
Washington, DC   20036
(202) 822-8200
website: www.vpc.org

The Violence Policy Center (VPC) is a nonprofit organization that aims to stop death and injury from firearms. VPC conducts research on gun violence in America and works to develop violence-reduction policies and proposals. VPC publishes studies on a range of gun-violence issues, including "Cash and Carry: How Concealed Carry Laws Drive Gun Industry Profits."

Bibliography

Books

Ben Agger and Timothy W. Luke, eds.	*Gun Violence and Public Life.* Boulder, CO: Paradigm Publishers, 2014.
Philip J. Cook and Kristin A. Goss	*The Gun Debate: What Everyone Needs to Know.* New York: Oxford University Press, 2014.
Clayton E. Cramer	*Armed America: The Remarkable Story of How and Why Guns Became as American as Apple Pie.* Nashville, TN: Nelson Current, 2009.
Tom Diaz	*The Last Gun: How Changes in the Gun Industry Are Killing Americans and What It Will Take to Stop It.* New York: The New Press, 2013.
Anthony K. Fleming	*Gun Policy in the United States and Canada: The Impact of Mass Murders and Assassinations on Gun Control.* New York: Continuum, 2012.
Alan Gottlieb and Dave Workman	*Shooting Blanks: Facts Don't Matter to the Gun Ban Crowd.* Bellevue, WA: Merril Press, 2011.
David B. Kopel	*The Truth About Gun Control.* New York: Encounter Books, 2013.
John R. Lott Jr.	*More Guns, Less Crime: Understanding Crime and Gun-Control Laws,* 3rd ed. Chicago: University of Chicago Press, 2010.

Scott Melzer — *Gun Crusaders: The NRA's Culture War*. New York: New York University Press, 2009.

Piers Morgan — *Shooting Straight: Guns, Gays, God, and George Clooney*. New York: Gallery Books, 2013.

Grover G. Norquist — *Leave Us Alone: Getting the Government's Hands Off Our Money, Our Guns, Our Lives*. New York: HarperCollins, 2009.

Brian Anse Patrick — *Rise of the Anti-Media: In-Forming America's Concealed Weapon Carry Movement*. Lanham, MD: Lexington Books, 2010.

Gerry Souter — *American Shooter: A Personal History of Gun Culture in the United States*. Washington, DC: Potomac Books, 2012.

Robert J. Spitzer — *The Politics of Gun Control*. Boulder, CO: Paradigm Publishers, 2012.

Daniel W. Webster, Jon S. Vernick, and Michael R. Bloomberg — *Reducing Gun Violence in America: Informing Policy with Evidence and Analysis*. Baltimore, MD: Johns Hopkins University Press, 2013.

Craig R. Whitney — *Living with Guns: A Liberal's Case for the Second Amendment*. New York: PublicAffairs, 2012.

Adam Winkler — *Gunfight: The Battle over the Right to Bear Arms in America*. New York: W.W. Norton, 2013.

Periodicals and Internet Sources

Doug Bandow   "Gun Rights and Liberty Go Hand in Hand," *Investor's Business Daily*, February 22, 2013.

Randy Barnett   "The Supreme Court's Gun Showdown," *Wall Street Journal*, June 29, 2010.

Trevor Burrus   "How Shameful Policies Increase America's Gun Violence," *Huffington Post*, January 30, 2013. www.huffingtonpost.com.

Ted Galen Carpenter   "Are Lax US Gun Laws Fueling Mexico's Drug Violence?," *National Interest*, March 11, 2011. www.nationalinterest.org.

Steve Chapman   "The Unconcealed Truth About Carrying Guns: What the Gun Control Lobby Doesn't Want You to Know," Reason.com, March 31, 2011.

C.J. Ciaramella   "Concealed Carry on Campus: Nowhere Is Perfectly Safe—Give the Kids a Fighting Chance," *Weekly Standard*, May 5, 2010.

Charles C.W. Cooke   "Norway and Gun Control: Gun Laws Do Not Hit Their Target," *National Review Online*, July 27, 2011. www.nationalreview.com.

Justin Cronin   "Confessions of a Liberal Gun Owner," *New York Times*, January 27, 2013.

Brian Doherty   "Gun Control Couldn't Have
                         Stopped It," *Reason*, April 2011.

Max Fisher   "A Land Without Guns: How Japan
                         Has Virtually Eliminated Shooting
                         Deaths," *Atlantic*, July 23, 2012.

Richard Florida   "The Geography of Gun Deaths,"
                         Atlantic, January 13, 2011.

Josh Horwitz   "How Aaron Alexis Passed a
                         Background Check and Bought a
                         Gun," *Huffington Post*, September 19,
                         2013. www.huffingtonpost.com.

Richard L.   "Protect the Second Amendment:
Johnson   Teach a Child to Shoot," *Human
                         Events*, September 28, 2011.
                         www.humanevents.com.

Katie Kieffer   "Let Women Carry Concealed
                         Firearms on Campus," Townhall.com,
                         January 27, 2014.

Louis Klarevas   "Closing the Gap: How to Reform
                         US Gun Laws to Prevent Another
                         Tucson," *New Republic*, January 13,
                         2011.

Titania Kumeh   "Do Guns and College Mix?," *Mother
                         Jones*, September 30, 2010.
                         www.motherjones.com.

Robert A. Levy   "A Libertarian Case for Expanding
                         Gun Background Checks," *New York
                         Times*, April 26, 2013.

Los Angeles Times "Guns and States' Rights," November 18, 2011.

John R. Lott Jr. "'Military-Style Weapons': Function, Not Cosmetics, Should Govern Gun Policy," *National Review Online*, July 27, 2012. www.nationalreview.com.

Clifford D. May "Thank You for Not Packing Heat," *National Review Online*, January 11, 2011. www.nationalreview.com.

James Moran "Moran's News Commentary: 'National Right-to-Carry' Act Is Irresponsible," *Falls Church News-Press*, November 16, 2011.

Michael A. Nutter and Charles H. Ramsey "Don't Ease Gun Permit Rules," *Philadelphia Inquirer*, December 4, 2011.

David Paulin "Second Amendment Culture Wars: Eastern Elites vs. Gun-Friendly Red States," *American Thinker*, March 13, 2011. www.americanthinker.com.

Mike Piccione "Back Door Gun Control and Fighting Back," *Human Events*, June 14, 2011. www.humanevents.com.

Gary C. Sackett "Common Sense Weapons Bill That Would Make Us Safer," *Salt Lake Tribune*, May 27, 2011.

Adam Serwer "A Gun Rights Case Liberals Wanted to Lose, Just Not Like This," *American Prospect*, June 28, 2010. www.prospect.org.

Ilya Shapiro and   "Using Guns to Protect Liberty,"
Josh Blackman   *Washington Times*, February 23, 2010.

Doug Thomson   "Another Gun Law Would Not Have
                       Saved Those in Tucson," *Capitol Hill
                       Blue*, January 12, 2011.
                       www.capitolhillblue.com.

USA Today   "Our View on Guns: Porous Laws
                       Help Lunatics Get Their Hands on
                       Deadly Weapons," January 11, 2011.

Adam Winkler   "The Secret History of Guns,"
                       Atlantic, September 2011.

Index